Startup... Just Startup

A Step by Step Guide on How to Become a Successful Entrepreneur

GAURAV VASISHTA

INDIA • SINGAPORE • MALAYSIA

Notion Press Media Pvt Ltd

No. 50, Chettiyar Agaram Main Road
Vanagaram, Chennai, Tamil Nadu – 600 095

First Published by Notion Press 2021
Copyright © Gaurav Vasishta 2021
All Rights Reserved.

ISBN 978-1-63850-569-3

This book has been published with all efforts taken to make the material error-free after the consent of the author. However, the author and the publisher do not assume and hereby disclaim any liability to any party for any loss, damage, or disruption caused by errors or omissions, whether such errors or omissions result from negligence, accident, or any other cause.

While every effort has been made to avoid any mistake or omission, this publication is being sold on the condition and understanding that neither the author nor the publishers or printers would be liable in any manner to any person by reason of any mistake or omission in this publication or for any action taken or omitted to be taken or advice rendered or accepted on the basis of this work. For any defect in printing or binding the publishers will be liable only to replace the defective copy by another copy of this work then available.

CONTENTS

Preface	*5*
1. Introduction To Entrepreneurship	7
2. The Correct Entrepreneurship Mindset	17
3. How to Get Ideas For Your Startup	28
4. How to Validate A Business Idea Through Feedback?	40
5. Business Plan	55
6. Business Risks You Must Be Aware of	69
7. Customer Journey Blueprint	81
8. Boost Productivity	92
9. Sales & Marketing	107
10. Digital Marketing	124
11. Protect Your Business & Ip	141
12. Fundraising	156
Tool List	*173*
Author Bio	*175*

PREFACE

"Start-up...Just Start-up!" is a complete guide and toolset for first-time and recurring entrepreneurs. You would be able to actually learn the art of entrepreneurship and build successful start-ups using this step-by-step guide. This book emphasises on building strong foundations and providing clarity of concept so that your business stands the pressures of time and be effective and profitable. It is a culmination of years of experience, learning and success – all squeezed into this wonderful and helpful guide for start-ups.

Entrepreneurship is not a destination, it's a journey. The journey of a start-up begins with a great innovative idea. This book takes you on this journey by getting you into the right mind-set. It works with you on your ideas and how to get them in the first place. Validation of your ideas would be the next step so that once you are making the business plans with me, your idea is already viable and validated. We shall understand the risks involved and focus on the potential customers and their personas. In this book, I will provide you solid tools to boost your productivity before you master sales and marketing, with a special chapter only for digital marketing. After lessons in productivity, sales and marketing, I will show you – how to protect your business and IP. Towards the end of our journey, you will master the art of raising funds and making your own effective pitch deck.

PREFACE

Having a start-up gives you freedom from predictability and the entire responsibility for its success lies with you. I do not promise that the journey would be easy. In fact, on the contrary, the journey would be akin to climbing a hill …and believe me, albeit, with difficulty, that hill can be climbed with passion, perseverance and persistence. And once you do climb it and get to the top, the view would be just spectacular!

Enjoy the read!

Chapter 1
INTRODUCTION TO ENTREPRENEURSHIP

I come from a very humble background. Being a teacher himself, my father gave me the most precious gift of my life – education. Armed with an engineering degree, I strutted around, proud of having achieved something. Getting a job was a grind, to keep the job was even worse. I thought, I was inadequate. In fact, people made me feel and believe that I was inadequate. Eventually, I fell for this pressure and enrolled for masters – yes! More studying, more loans, more burden for the family. Started working part time to make ends meet. From pizza maker to dish washer to berry picker – did it all! It was while berry picking that I met some Thai workers seeking a better European dream. And out of long sessions of vodka in the cold Swedish nights, was born the idea of my first start-up – Homework! Cleaning homes with the help of the Thai workers. Clean, earn, return. It was a hustle. My body shivered with excitement on every order. Butterflies pranced in my stomach when something went wrong – I was excited, I was alive!!!

I became an Entrepreneur.

So, who is an entrepreneur? The creator of a new business, courageous risk taker, who generates wealth, growth and innovation, while enjoying most of the rewards. Entrepreneurs play a key role in the economy, bringing innovative ideas to the market, ideas that solve a real need, using all the necessary skills and initiative required. Entrepreneurs create their own definition of success based on values that matter to them.

So, what makes an entrepreneur? Well, it is a combination of a lot of things. I became one by accident and necessity. What about you? Lets run a quick test on you to see if you have it in you to become an entrepreneur ……ready?

Tool 1: Do you have what it takes to be an entrepreneur? Test yourself.

1. **You like to stick it to your "boss"**

    If you feel like sending an email to your boss or imagine sending one to your previous boss which really and truly would be like "sticking it to the boss", well you are getting warmed up to become an entrepreneur. It feels amazing! It would be something that you would wrestle with for a while, a lot of doubt about financial security and the fear of potentially falling flat on your face – all that will come into play. But, if you ever did make the decision to quit, once and for all, you would never look back!

2. **You like to Work on Your Own Schedule**

    Most people will have something on their schedules. But, having the ability to dictate when you work, when you'll be in office and, when you would be available for meetings is a freedom that you simply want! You can't do that working for someone else.

3. **You would like to work where You Like**

    In this new Covid-19 era, most days I work at home. But let's just throw Covid-19 out of the picture for a second – would you not like to work from anywhere you want? Sometimes on the beach, garden or on more realistic days from a coffee shop. Being location independent is the key.

4. **You would like to choose and work with people You Like**

   One of the major benefits of being an entrepreneur, is the ability to be able to pick and choose who you work with and do business with. You would get to team-up with the right people and that is the master-key to a happy working relationship.

5. **You would like to create Your Own Opportunities**

   They say opportunity does not knock twice …but what if you were creating them left, right and centre? As your own boss, you would have the ability to create your own opportunities by doing things like attending any event, networking with like-minded people and much more.

6. **You want to develop Products & Services You Love**

   Wouldn't it be great if you could say that you believed in, and thoroughly loved every product and service you've produced for your companies? Being passionate about something is great – to work on your passion is the greatest feeling of them all!

7. **You want to "Make a Difference"**

   The best and the only way to make a difference is by solving a problem for someone, or a company. Identify the real "need" of the people and find a solution for it, and you'll enjoy success. People want to do business with people that help them or their cause. Be that person!

8. **Be your Own Boss**

   CEO. Sounds good right? But the real meaning of CEO is Chief Effort Officer!!! Being the boss feels good, but it comes with its challenges. Just remember point 1 and you will realize how important it is to be a good leader. Boss is just a term – be a good leader and inspire, then you'll be just fine.

9. **You want to Stand Up for What You Believe In and bring a change**

   Being an entrepreneur also gives you the chance to stand up for what you believe in, and bring in change. You always have to keep in mind that it is one thing to be more productive and successful but a totally another feeling to have the ability to change people's perceptions about how things should be.

10. **Respect**

    In this day and age 'introduction' is everything. Society judges you at every nook and corner by your status. You yearn to be respected, more so by your family and friends. No better introduction than the owner of your own company. Entrepreneur, the risk taker, the contributor to the economy and job creation, is respected. Period!

So, if you relate to any of the above 10 points then look no further! You have come to the right place. I have squeezed my 22 years of entrepreneurial experience and learning in this book. I ensure you, during this journey, I will give you all the tools along with a step-by-step roadmap to turn your business idea into a profitable business.

Even if you are an absolute beginner, this book will guide you to successfully plan and start your business. You might be building your first business, unsure and probably scared ...but you are not alone. Millions of first-time entrepreneurs feel that way, and that's exactly how I felt when I started my first company "Homework" 22 years ago. I've felt the stress you might be feeling, and I've been through the hardships you might face or are facing. The great news is that I'll walk you through each step for starting your business from selecting the best business idea, to business planning, raising money, and starting your business with absolute correct fundamentals to give your business the best chance to succeed. The best hack if there ever was!!!

INTRODUCTION TO ENTREPRENEURSHIP

By the end of this book, you will no longer be one of thousands of "wantapreneurs." You will have taken your first positive steps to business success. You will become a strong and independent entrepreneur. You'll know exactly where you are going in business and how you are going to get there. You will be able to make correct and confident decisions. Use this book as a step-by-step entrepreneurship guide to turn your business ideas into a successful business.

> "The best part of being an entrepreneur is contributing something larger than yourself. Entrepreneurs solve problems and bring a product or service to the world that people need. Sure, you have the opportunity to get paid well, but giving livelihood to others and crafting the world you want to see is way more fulfilling."
>
> – Matt Wilson, co-founder, Under30Experiences

Image by Gerd Altmann from Pixabay

So, let's get straight into it! Ever wondered what are the entrepreneurship skills you must know?

Like I have said before, entrepreneurship is not a destination, it's a journey. On this journey, there is no finish line and neither is there any expectation of arriving at one. The journey is all about small achievements and small goals. If you reach a milestone, do stop and enjoy the moment. I am not saying that you shouldn't have expectations as that is what pushes you to step outside of your comfort zone and grow. The idea is to have the ability to stretch yourself into doing things that truly help your business experience. On any journey, you have moments of joy interspersed with more than a few setbacks, the classic crest and trough scenario. During the highs, you feel like you can accomplish anything and the sky is the limit. Use the highs to derive strength and motivation and always comprehend the success formula that helps your business. During the lows, negativity and frustration can easily take over. You need to have the ability to understand the ups and downs and reflect on the positives and what worked. Adverse environments bring out the best work and innovation. Work harder and wiser when down.

The journey will be exciting as it would surprise you whenever you are sitting on your laurels and give you unexpected twists and turns. From the inception of the idea to seeing it become the next big thing, your exploration never ends. Three words that I am going to use a few times in this book are going to be passion, perseverance and persistence, make these words the cornerstones of your entrepreneurial journey.

Tool 2: Must have Skills of an Entrepreneur:

It is not easy to write about the skills a person must possess as each of us are unique in our own way and personalities. However, there are certain skills that can definitely be made part of our quiver so that we are prepared to shoot the right arrows when the time comes.

Here is a go-to skill set that probably you already possess and if not, could be inculcated, to nudge you ahead in seeing your idea to fruition.

- **Decisive and Innovative** – Decisiveness is one of the most important skills entrepreneurs need. Being decisive means being able to make decisions firmly and swiftly, rather than procrastinating. Ability to innovate is what gets you started in the first place, so keep developing solutions that transform your ideas into practical reality.

- **Leadership and Teamwork** – An entrepreneur creates an organization from an idea. Sounds great, but you need to develop the qualities of a leader. Sooner than later you would be working with a team. Teamwork is based on inclusive growth and as a leader, your job is to ensure that your team is motivated and works for the same beliefs and goals that you started with.

- **Time-Management** – It is essential to have time management and organizational skills as you will find out the hard way that there is always too much to be done. Learn to break down tasks into manageable to-do lists and set deadlines and achievable objectives for yourself and your team. Meticulous prioritization, defined milestones, execution, and iteration are all important.

- **Efficiency** – Resources would be limited, so you must have the efficiency to make the best possible use of them. An entrepreneur must recognise and implement the most effective way of doing a task. By improving efficiency, a business can reduce its costs and improve its competitiveness.

- **Communication and Networking** – Every entrepreneur needs to be an effective communicator. From active listening during discussions to promoting awareness of your brand, communication skills are a must. One major by-product of communication skills is networking, which would involve establishing and developing long-term relations with like-minded people. Effective communication and networking helps you to feel the pulse of the market, trends and meet prospective customers, partners, and mentors.

- **Sales Marketing and Branding** – Get used to these three skills as you would be using them in your sleep. **Branding** is about who you are and how you present yourself and your values. **Marketin**g is how you communicate your brand to your potential customers. **Sales** is the final step in the process which brings the essential money to your business. I have a complete chapter on sales and marketing and a separate chapter on digital marketing, which would be highly relevant for you.

- **Strategy and Planning** – Strategic direction is necessary for you to understand where you are trying to get in the long term, where and how you would be competitive, what resources would you require at each stage and how would you be representing your values to all your stakeholders. Planning would allow you to take decisive actions to achieve the business goals while utilizing the available resources optimally and effectively.

- **Flexible learning** – The ability to learn and improve is one of the most important skills that you must have as an entrepreneur. This is also the essence of this book that *entrepreneurship can be learnt.* You have the ultimate luxury of freedom and choice as to when, how, what and where you want to learn different skills necessary to become a successful entrepreneur. Don't ever be infected by the "I know it all" bug. You will need to constantly upgrade and update yourself with changing circumstances. And the best way to counter contingencies and situations is through knowledge. Remember that failures are often the best learning experiences, so never give up and keep absorbing information, knowledge and expertise. Keep learning!

For me, being an entrepreneur has been a stimulating and liberating endeavour. It has not been an easy voyage but the sense of achievement is so gratifying, that I want to encourage and motivate you to take this cruise of a lifetime. So many of you will have ideas for a business or a product, all you need to do is create a plan, learn the basics and take the leap to build your own start-up.

This first chapter is all about getting you a feel of what it would take to become an entrepreneur by giving you a checklist to see if you are cut out to be an entrepreneur. It will then give you an idea of the skills required to be successful. Some of you might be introverts and may not be aware of the wonderful abilities you have, while some of you would already be sure of doing exceptionally well in your entrepreneurial journey. All in all, there is some good news for everyone! And I have said this before, entrepreneurship can be learned! This book can be used as an effective learning tool for entrepreneurship.

Tip: Use the Tool Index to go back to the part you need help with at different stages on your entrepreneurial journey.

> *"Rise up and shine like a pole star amidst the waves and storms of life while living in the present and making it pleasant"*
>
> *– K.K. Sharma, Mentor & motivational Guru*

20 Most Famous Entrepreneurs of Modern Age

- 1. Jeff Bezos - AMAZON
- 2. Bill Gates - MICROSOFT
- 3. Mark Zuckerberg - FACEBOOK
- 4. Larry Page & Sergey Brin - GOOGLE
- 5. Richard Branson - VIRGIN GROUP
- 6. Steve Jobs - APPLE
- 7. Larry Ellison - ORACLE
- 8. Travis Kalanick - UBER
- 9. Kevin Systrom - INSTAGRAM
- 10. Elon Musk - PAYPAL/SPACEX/TESLA
- 11. Steve Ballmer - MICROSOFT
- 12. Reid Hoffman - LINKEDIN
- 13. Oprah Winfrey - OPRAH WINFREY
- 14. Jack Dorsey - TWITTER
- 15. Ray Dalio - BRIDGEWATER
- 16. Jack Ma - ALIBABA
- 17. Brian Chesky - AIRBNB
- 18. Adam D'Angelo - QUORA
- 19. Ratan Tata - TATA GROUP
- 20. Ben Silbermann - PINTEREST

Chapter 2
THE CORRECT ENTREPRENEURSHIP MINDSET

While the last chapter was about preparing you for the journey ahead, you actually start from here to build the correct entrepreneurship mindset. It is just a way of thinking that equips you to be decisive, overcome challenges and accept responsibility for your outcomes. The right mindset would enable you to develop the ability to improve your skills, learn from your mistakes, and work effectively on your innovations and ideas. It can be summed up in one of the great historical quote:

> "Do what you can with what you have, where you are"
> – Theodore Roosevelt.

Image by Chenspec from Pixabay

It is of upmost importance to know the truth to three aspects of your life that only you have the answer to – WHO? WHAT? WHOM?

Time to start introspecting and laying the foundation to understand yourself. Time to pick up a sheet of paper and make a chart to know the real you. If you really want to be successful as an entrepreneur, just take my word and start jotting down on three pieces of information. Know yourself first then start.

***Tool 3: Know Yourself Chart** – it starts here*

Sheet 1 - Who Am I

I remember a Jackie Chan movie of the same name but this is far from it. More fun surely. So, write down on a sheet your answers to the following questions:

a. What is my background?

b. What legacy do I have?

c. How much money do I actually have which I can afford to lose?

d. What do I have that would make me valuable in a team?
e. What am I passionate about?
f. What makes me Unique?
g. What would I do if I did not have to work for money?
h. What are my hobbies/interests?

After Sheet 1 is filled, let's get to Sheet 2, which is – 'What I know?'

Sheet 2 - What I Know?

a. What Education, vocation or other skills do I have?
b. What are my experiences in life that have shaped me?
c. What knowledge do I have that is of value to others?
d. Am I good at something? What makes me better than others?
e. What am I known for among my family and friends?
f. Do I have any skillset that people would pay for?
g. Have I worked and gained experience in a company or domain?

Sheet 3 - Whom I know?

a. Where I have worked, like ever – all work?
b. List the companies, small scale or big – where I know people?
c. Family – yes! List the lost uncles and nieces and what they do?
d. Friends – List the lost ones too, and what they do?
e. Acquaintances – list them all and what they do?
f. Common beliefs – are there any people I would love to do business with? List them.

g. People I could meet but have avoided as I feel awkward?

h. Folks I feel would be of great benefit to my start-up if I collaborated with them? This is if you already have an idea.

Image by Gerd Altmann from Pixabay

> *"The mindset is much more important than having a million dollars."*
>
> *– Justin Ho, How To Develop A Million Dollar Mindset*

Know your means:

In this book, you would be given a lot of information and tools relevant to succeed in the start-up space, from how to get ideas to raising money and making a pitch deck. No tool is more important than the one above and jotting down for perspective the three basic questions "Who? What? Whom?" in form of a chart would empower you tremendously. The reason, I emphasize the importance of knowing yourself first is that you always start with your means. No point dreaming about things that might happen. Be honest to yourself and things will start to fall in place. Lie to yourself and you will live a lie ...forever!

Don't take shortcuts. The point here, and I did call it a Tool, is to understand who you are, your means, yourself, what you know, your expertise and whom you know. This is the starting point – get this right, the understanding of your means, and you have the foundation to honestly understand whether you would be able to make it as an entrepreneur. Why do I call it the foundation? Because if you start here, you will always know what your entire worth is – be honest and it will not bite you in the back

The point is to start with your means. You cannot start a company by setting your success strategy based on the size of funds you raise. Nor is raising funds the benchmark to you being successful. Believe me that you have been lied to and fed false information all this while. A successful company is sustainable. Start with your means and start with the principle of affordable loss and you will never face failure.

Failure is just expectations not being met – lower the expectations and you never fail.

Tool 4: The Right Mindset for Success

It's so easy to think that having a start-up is cool and easy. Shows like Shark Tank glamorize the start-ups and give unrealistic aspirations and dreams. To be successful, however, you need to have the right mindset and a strong foundation and thought process that would make you confident, decisive and positive. Entrepreneurs who lack decisiveness and confidence or those who have a pessimistic mindset seldom succeed. So how does one get the right mindset?

Through a disciplined approach and imbibing basic traits and qualities. I will give you the tool, you are the one who has to work on it. The promise I make is that, if you do follow the basics and incorporate the right mindset, success will come calling sooner than you think. So here are 9 strategic qualities you need to develop for the right mindset:

1. **Don't procrastinate:**

    If you have an idea, the best time to start working on it is now. Procrastination often leads to missed opportunities. How many times, when you see a successful start-up, have you said to your friends "hey, even I had thought of that!" When an opportunity presents itself, don't wait until you can get yourself out of your comfort zone, cause you and I both know, that ain't going to happen. You have an idea, you start developing and working on it as soon as you can. This standard mind-set holds true for other decisions and other work opportunities too. Entrepreneurship is all about problem solving, so you need to be solving the problem at hand and not just thinking you would do it one day. Get up!

2. **Affordable Loss:**

    Saras Sarasvathy's theory of Effectuation (2001) describes an approach to making decisions and performing actions in entrepreneurship processes, where you identify the next best step by assessing the resources available to achieve your goals, while continuously balancing these goals with your resources and actions. I got the opportunity to teach this recently and fell in love with the concept. I had been doing it practically throughout my journey as an entrepreneur, but never had put it down as theory before. Affordable loss theory or investing only as much as you are willing to lose gives you relief from stress and failure. Earlier, when I covered starting with your means, this is exactly what I was referring to. Know your means and what you can afford to lose and no start-up would ever be a failure.

3. **Failure as a Learning:**

   Failure for me is an integral part of the learning process. Failure often leads to discovery and innovation if you can know, accept and move on from it. Every time you face an adverse situation and an outcome that did not meet your expectations, redefine it, analyze it and work on what you think could have been done to change the outcome. Clarity of concept is the key here with an open mind to change what you might be doing wrong. Don't sit on failures with regret, but work on what they taught you and apply the lessons learnt.

4. **Be open to advice and mentors:**

   I have really benefitted from working with mentors when I was less experienced and have built a positive mindset in the process. Being open to advice helps you find dependable, engaged and authentic people willing to help you in your pursuit of success. There is a long list of benefits of getting genuine advice, not limited to, guidance, emotional support, motivation, setting goals, developing contacts and identifying resources. While choosing an advisor or a mentor, look for someone who is a good fit for you, is enthusiastic, and hopefully, an expert in their field.

5. **Create a morning routine:**

   The most productive period of your day is the first two to three hours of your morning. A great way to start a day is to create momentum for the entire day by making a list of everything you are looking forward to do. Tackle the most difficult tasks first and the rest of the day seems to blow by like a breeze. A morning routine can give you time to focus on yourself in ways that you might have otherwise found difficult. Routine is a strong word that cannot be taken lightly, as it requires loads of discipline. Be disciplined and focus on the positives around you.

6. **Vision and Goals:**

    Goals make the journey fun as there would be some anticipation and enthusiasm created in the process. To have a vision is like having a destination that you want to achieve, on an unknown path. Goals would act as milestones and set the path for the deserved achievement of your vision. Your experiences would help you learn and adapt but set goals for results, skills, knowledge, training etc. to keep you focused and on track. Remember to keep the goals time bound and achievable.

7. **Follow Your Passion:**

    Maybe the most common advice you ever hear is 'follow your passion'. Is it a good one? Let's investigate. There are two kinds of motivation – intrinsic and extrinsic. Intrinsic motivation is the one that comes from inside. It's the long-lasting motivation. Extrinsic motivations are the short-term highs you experience through outer mediums like listening to a great energetic song or eating that delightful piece of pie. Needless to say, your intrinsic motivation a-la-passion is the one which lasts longer and should be pursued. You need passion for sustenance. Keep your passion on leash and prepare a plan before making the jump.

8. **Listen to your Instincts:**

    Your gut instinct or your intuition in the purest form is almost always correct, but they often get corrupted with your thoughts and doubts. We were discussing procrastination and following your passion, both of these are dependent upon your instincts. Pay attention to what goes on around you, connect with people, feel, let the bad feelings go and then trust your gut feeling.

Instincts evolve as you believe, and if you believe, everything is possible.

9. **Have Gratitude:**

    One of the emotions I consider the most positive, is gratitude. It is about being appreciative and thankful for what we have rather than dwell on the negatives. Take a pause, a pause to notice the relations, things and lifestyle we often take for granted. The world would seem a much better place and your negativity would disappear if you embrace the magic of gratitude. I am thankful for whatever I have achieved in life, my family, friends and the opportunities that came my way. I am thankful that I got the chance to write down my learning, experience and knowledge in this book and share them with you.

I recently came across this excerpt from a speech at a McKinsey internal meeting in 1990 by John W Gardner. It is counted as one of the most influential business speeches and has a lot to teach us:

"The things you learn in maturity aren't simple things such as acquiring information and skills.

You learn not to engage in self-destructive behavior.

You learn not to burn up energy in anxiety.

You discover how to manage your tensions.

You learn that self-pity and resentment are among the most toxic of drugs.

You find that the world loves talent but pays off on character.

You come to understand that most people are neither for you nor against you; they are thinking about themselves.

You learn that no matter how hard you try to please, some people in this world are not going to love you, a lesson that is at first troubling and then really quite relaxing.

Those are things that are hard to learn early in life. As a rule, you have to have picked up some mileage and some dents in your fenders before you understand.

This too shall pass. As we approach another year, let's have the maturity to understand and relax, to manage our tensions and be bothered by things which really matter and stay blessed forever".

Amazingly true perspective and I shared it as it motivates and helps build the right mindset for an entrepreneur. Having the correct mindset would not only help you in your entrepreneurial journey but would also benefit you by giving you a better quality of life, higher energy levels, empathy and better time and stress management skills. Once we have the right mindset, now we can start working on the ideas, how to get them and work on them in the next chapter.

> "The origin of innovation and entrepreneurship is a creative mindset"
>
> – Michael Harris Phd

THE CORRECT ENTREPRENEURSHIP MINDSET

Quotes from Famous Entrepreneurs you will love

- 1. "I'm convinced that about half of what separates successful entrepreneurs from the nonsuccessful ones is pure perseverance." Steve Jobs, co-founder of Apple Inc.
- 2. "Vision is something you see and others don't. Some people would say that's a pocket definition of lunacy. But it also defines entrepreneurial spirit. "Anita Roddick, founder of The BodyShop
- 3. "Ideas are cheap. Ideas are easy. Ideas are common. Everybody has ideas. Ideas are highly, highly overvalued. Execution is all that matters." Casey Neistat, Filmmaker and tech entrepreneur
- 4. "Be ready to revise any system, scrap any method, abandon any theory, if the success of the job requires it." Henry Ford, founder of the Ford Motor Company
- 5. "Failure is an option here. If things are not failing, you are not innovating enough. "Elon Musk, founder and CEO of Tesla Inc. and SpaceX
- 6. "One of the only ways to get out of a tight box is to invent your way out." Jeff Bezos, CEO of Amazon
- 7. "I think it is often easier to make progress on mega-ambitious dreams. Since no one else is crazy enough to do it, you have little competition." Larry Page, co-founder of Google
- 8. "Players should never fight. A real businessman or entrepreneur has no enemies. Once he understands this, the sky's the limit. "Jack Ma, co-founder of Alibaba
- 9. "If we tried to think of a good idea, we wouldn't have been able to think of a good idea at all. You just have to have a solution for a problem in your own life. "Brian Chesky, co-founder of Airbnb
- 10. "If you've got an idea, start today. There's no better time than now to get going. That doesn't mean quit your job and jump into your idea 100% from day one, but there's always small progress that can be made to start the movement." Kevin Systrom, co-founder of Instagram

Chapter 3
HOW TO GET IDEAS FOR YOUR STARTUP

Idea! That's how any great venture starts. The one idea, that one epiphany that an entrepreneur has, that makes them realize they want to make a business out of it. Some people believe that the 'Idea' itself is the Start-up. Although, I do not share their belief, for me the idea is the foundation on which the pillars of planning and implementation are constructed to shape the organization. But even I can't deny the significance of an idea in the whole entrepreneurial journey. It is the launchpad that starts the journey. There have been numerous articles, videos and podcasts that cover the important features that an idea should have and how to shape your idea for the market. The web is almost saturated with these resources and going through them can be quite tiring and sometimes even intimidating. So, I decided to handpick the best resources available out there and curate it into this one master chapter. In this chapter, I will cover the insights I found most useful and practical in my research.

Image by Elisa Reva from Pixabay

Tool 5: How to Get Ideas for Your Start-up

To start on How to get ideas for your startup, let us first understand why startups fail. There was an interesting research by CB Insights that gave the top twenty reasons for the failure of startups. You would be surprised to learn that the number 1 reason for failure of startups is "NO MARKET NEED". Shocking right? So why start with an idea that has no market need? We have to be prudent enough to understand that in our heads the idea might sound good, but it needs to pass a simple test of having a market need. If your idea is not solving any problem and need of the market, then it is already a fused bulb idea. Junk it. Don't convince yourself to believe in stuff that won't be required by the market. On the other hand, I am hardly discouraging you. I am just asking you to be smart about the idea you choose. In the movie Cocktail, Tom Cruise's character, Brian Flanagan, tells the story of the man who invented the plastic tips that go on the ends of shoelaces (aka Flugelbinders). This man created something so simple but is now insanely wealthy. Brian/Cruise wants to find his flugelbinder idea and make a fortune. An idea can be as simple as a shoelace binder, it just needs to address a market need.

So, we now know that we need to be solving a problem and must address a market need, in addition we must be innovative. So, what is this innovation? Just think of it as an introduction of new organizational structures, new markets, new channels, new methods, new products or services. *Let's define innovation as something that creates value and effectively transfers this value to the market.* If you become an entrepreneur, you become a part of an ecosystem that forces change and innovation in the market.

So, you have to be addressing a need, solving a problem and also be innovative. Wow, that's simple! But it does not end there. You have to be creating products or services that become essential for your customers. The challenge to find that brilliant idea seems to get tougher and tougher. To relieve your discomfort, I would like to point out that the big recent successful start-ups have all come after addressing a need, solving a problem and being innovative – Uber, AirBnB, Instagram, Whatsapp and the list is endless. None of the founders of these companies could have ever imagined that they would turn out so right or so big ......but they did. What worked in their favor, apart from being in the right place at the right time, are points I started out with – create value out of solving a problem, must be a need and be creative/innovative doing it!

Then let me come to what we see around us – competition. Do you really think there were no other e-commerce companies when Amazon or Flipkart came around? Infact, there were thousands of start-ups who had the exact same idea! So, is originality so important? Not really. Effective execution holds the key to success. Of course, I repeat, it does help to be in the right place at the right time, so always network and understand the importance of not being confined to your own little world – venture out. More on competition, I kinda denounce the idea that competition should be our worry. In my book, if they are doing good, then they are winners. Instead of looking at the winners and worrying, one should learn from them. The problem is we go overboard in adulation, while the truth is that one must admire in moderation. If you admire them for winning then you would start copying them instead of learning from them and getting better.

Coming to the business conglomerates like Amazon and Google and their monopoly over the market. We should think about monopoly as a good thing…why? Well, it certainly is. From the point of view of a founder or entrepreneur, you want your company to always be a monopoly, you want to be offering something to the world that no one else is offering and that therefore you'll have some really healthy profit margins around your business. So, from the inside, I would argue monopoly is always a good thing and that's what every entrepreneur should attempt to build from the point of view of society as a whole. But there is an artificial scarcity created by the monopolies. Monopoly is broken by innovation and new ways. I admire Google for doing the same in the 90s. Google shouldn't have existed, well, it always has. It sure was always a question in what dimension was Google really new or really different. I would argue that with Google and the search business it was the PageRank algorithm which was the innovation. It was the way to automate search and computerize it that was quite new and that fundamentally transformed search into this vastly bigger space than anyone had thought it was in the 90s. I would say, Facebook was the first one to really crack the code on making personal identity real.

So now we know the basic foundations of finding that million-dollar idea. We must consider the turmoil in our minds when it comes to talking about generating value and making profits. It can be said that an entrepreneur should aim to generate value to the society and then try to capture a small fraction of that value for himself. I think, it is true for any great company, you have to build something that is valuable to the world and you need to capture some fraction of what you create. So, the fundamentals are that you have to create X dollars in value and you have to get Y percent of X. The problem, with innovators is that in most cases Y is about zero percent. This is the actual disturbing element in the history of innovation that a lot of innovators discovered things but weren't able to get anything. Remember, Tesla was out competed by Edison even though Edison had an inferior technology. Tesla became a famous brand name because of another entrepreneur, but that is another story.

Let me give some examples. The one which comes to mind immediately for sure success is the software industry. As we dwell on the software industry, you will notice that the marginal cost of creating software is next to nothing but due to the economy of the scales, software industry is one of the most profitable ones. We can easily predict another digital revolution some decades down the line due to the growing monopoly of some software companies.

Talking about the hottest topic related to new ventures – luck. It's always a very important question in business to know what is the role of chance and how much is everything just a matter of luck. One way or the other, luck does play a very important role, so it's a very hard question to answer because we can never run this experiment twice. But I think it's always good to have some sort of a plan to be present at the right places at the right time. If we do not venture out, luck will never be on our side. I would like to think like a venture capitalist – when I invest in businesses, I treat them as lottery tickets. If you start thinking – *"Okay, I don't know if this is going to work … maybe it works, maybe it won't. I'll give them some money"*, and do that a bunch of times you have kind of already psyched yourself into losing money. Personally, I do much better when I have really high conviction and am willing to put a lot of the capital behind an idea. Whereas, when I'm saying that it's a lottery ticket I'm actually too lazy to really think about the strengths and weaknesses of a given business. So even though there is such a thing as luck and it's quite important in some ways, I think we exaggerate its importance and often when we use the word luck we should instead just be thinking a little bit harder.

We must also consider the topic and the importance of college and the 'one size fits all' approach to education. This is something I strongly feel about. So please bear with me and understand what I am trying to say. I feel this one size fits all approach is ineffective. The importance of college and traditional education depends on the individual. I don't think everyone should go to college. I surely don't think everyone should drop out of college and start a company. I think in terms of what we do with our lives with our careers there's no right answer. My two bits and golden advice is that you should be following your passion and making your own way. Generating value for society through your Idea is the biggest takeaway from this. An idea, in itself is nothing if not converted into reality.

I still remember, Mr Ronak Samantray, in his Tedx talk, spoke about his journey from quitting Microsoft to co-founding 'NowFloats' with three cofounders. Through his journey, he told us about how ideas can be converted to reality. NowFloats, an innovative start-up, that aims to make internet relevant for India's innumerable small businesses. He emphasised on being illogical. He said that you should be in absolute love with your Idea and like all the things in love be ready to do anything for it. He claimed that the whole world of entrepreneurship is crazy and illogical. No logical mind would quit his job security for an idea that might fail. He said that one should trust their gut. "If you have Butterflies…Jump". I would like to add, if you love your idea then jump and act on it.

Now let me come to the team. I must mention here the great importance of having the right team to get the job done. You should always respect your team and make them believe that the idea behind the start-up is their own by developing a sense of ownership in them. So that they give their all to "their" idea.

Another thing, I almost find it ridiculous the notion of hiding the idea. In this world of billions of people someone else surely has the exact same idea. So do not try to hide it. Announce your idea and in doing so earn the trust and respect of your team and business associates. If you feel that you have it all figured out then you are wrong. To have this notion that you know all the answers is fundamentally wrong and you should always be on the lookout for better answers and opportunities. I must emphasize, always remember the "Why?" of why you started this venture. It will keep you motivated and keep you from giving up. The biggest takeaway from it should be that you should love your idea, to have a team and believe that you will make it. We will later get into the specifics of planning and executing but I believe this is quite an interesting journey through the spirit of entrepreneurship.

Even if you have a great idea, success is far from assured. That's because for every great idea that has shaped our world there are thousands of seemingly great ideas that have flopped. In order to succeed, a great business idea needs a great business model and they're not the same thing. Even if customers love your value proposition you can fail if your business model is not scalable and financially sustainable. You need to find reliable channels, to reach and acquire your customers. You need to build an infrastructure that won't collapse as your business begins to grow. Failing to do just one of these things can mean death to your business however great your idea is, that's why your first work is to search for the right business model to map this world of challenges so it can be tamed and organized, allowing you to explore it, manage it and plan for it. You need to account for threats and competitions. We will cover the business model and planning in the coming chapters.

See, the only judge of an idea is your future customer. What you've created so far is just hypotheses, meaning they are just guesses that need to be true. For your idea to succeed, you have to test these hypotheses, whether they fail or succeed. Learn, then adjust – this process is known as **Customer Development and Lean Start-up**. Get out into the world and see if you're right. You can conduct low-cost experiments to test your most important hypotheses. Talk to your potential partners and industry experts but most importantly talk to your prospective customers, as they're likely to have questions and concerns that never crossed your mind. What you learn in the field, can also lead you to unexpected opportunities. This might lead you to modify your original idea in favour of something new. As you gain confidence with your idea you should intensify testing. You will succeed in some ways but you will fail in others. Because there will always be factors that you can't foresee from your position. If you adapt rapidly and cheaply you can account for these factors and find solutions. And once you have modified and adjusted your ideas, you can have confidence in it. Now, after a little bit of validation, if you pitch it to investors, there is a much higher probability of success than from when you started.

The biggest takeaway from this is to have your ideas organised which will lead to many new breakthroughs that you might not have foreseen yourself.

So now let's start winding down to the reality and start evaluating a business idea. How do we come up with and evaluate start-up ideas? This may seem pretty basic but the fact is no matter how hard you work on an idea, if the idea is not good it's not going to work. So I think, a lot of time and effort should be spent talking about how to evaluate ideas. So let me simplify this for you. Here is a list of some questions an entrepreneur must ask to gauge the true validity of his/her idea.

- **Do people actually want this?** This may seem very obvious and a very basic thing to say but the number one reason a start-up doesn't work is because people don't want the product that start-up is making.
- **Has anyone tried this before?** Often, the start-ups do no research whatsoever about who has tried their idea before and if they were successful or unsuccessful. When I talk to a founder about their company, I always

ask if there are any competitors. If they say, no one has ever done this before they're probably either wrong or crazy. Most likely, people have tried it before and there's a lot to learn from the prior efforts. So you should definitely be asking yourself this and try to really take to heart the lessons from the folks that have tried before when you're evaluating a start-up idea. If really no one has tried it before then there's a good chance that people don't actually want it.

- **Why are YOU the team to do it?** Often, start-ups are founded by people that just want to start a company for the sake of doing it and they have no particular expertise or insight into the things they're working on. This is going to be tough because there's a good chance those founders don't know more than the average Jill on the street about that problem. It's really great, when you have a team that has very specific insights into what problem they're trying to solve. If you have a team like that, you are on the path to success. Even better if your team is also the customer of the product and they're just building a product to scratch their own itch. I find this as a good thing to do.

- **Why are you excited about working on this?** You may notice sometimes, people are just trying to start a start-up for the sake of doing it or because they think it's a cool thing to do. People may think, they came up with an idea but the problem is that they aren't particularly attached to it. They are already contemplating its failure. Whereas, when you talk to someone who's truly excited about what they're doing, it's contagious, and you can get the sense that even if a lot of roadblocks are put in front of the founder they're so excited and passionate about their idea they will overcome all that adversity. The fact is when you plan a start-up people are going to reject and humiliate you. You may have to hear 'no' on a daily basis. The world is going to tell you you're wrong. So, if you aren't excited about your idea there's absolutely no way that you're going to have the wherewithal to make it successful.

Image by Arek Socha from Pixabay

Have a simple communication of the idea. It is a myth that there is a connection between the funds raised and the success of a start-up. The way a lot of people think about start-ups is that the scorecard for who is successful and who is not successful is who raises the most money and how people on the outside valuate if something is working or not. The notion that a successful start-up is the one that raise money is simply untrue. The amount of money you raise and the press reports and articles that you read about all this great stuff happening does not give you an insight into how the product is working and its success. I would call fundraising a trailing indicator of the product/service of the company hitting milestones. The fact is when you talk to founders (and I myself have been a founder and raised many rounds of funding) it actually gets harder every time you raise money because the stakes are raised and because the size your company gets bigger and sometimes it gets even harder to grow when you raise money. So it's really important to separate the two elements in your own mind as a potential founder. There is a big difference between truly being successful, making a product/service that people want, and just trying to raise money. Real success versus external success.

So I would like you to evaluate the validity of an idea and in the process modify your idea to make it more exciting and attractive, both for the investors and to the customers and thus increase your overall probability of success.

It is very important that the founders find an idea that suits them. Find your strengths that would give you a competitive edge, but never lose sight of and always fix your weaknesses. Think of yourselves and make your own path following what you love.

Now, finally let me quickly talk about the importance of research and homework before starting a business venture. Ask yourself, "is there a strong need for my idea and does my product/service already exist?" For the new innovation-based businesses, their product ideas being first is critical but for most businesses improvising on an existing model might equally work. The true way to start a business is to understand your competition.

Getting an Idea for your start-up is the first step into the entrepreneurial world. The way ahead is as intimidating as it is exciting. I hope you found this chapter helpful and practical. I hope this makes your journey a little less daunting.

> *"Good ideas are common – what's uncommon are people who'll work hard enough to bring them about."*
>
> *– Ashleigh Brilliant*

HOW TO GET IDEAS FOR YOUR STARTUP

Some Great Ideas for a New Startup

- 1. Create a Food Waste Solution
- 2. Plant-Based or Non-processed Foods
- 3. Sell Zero-Waste Products that solve a need
- 4. Make Specialized Products for Pets
- 5. Create Custom Clothing or Accessories
- 6. Online Coaching or Offer Specialized Courses
- 7. Make a Smart Appliance
- 8. Tap Into Virtual Reality Experiences
- 9. Reinvent Exercising or New Age Fitness Solutions
- 10. Eco-Friendly, Health-Friendly Makeup and Beauty Products
- 11. Start a Business for Organizing
- 12. Vocational Skills Solutions and Consultations
- 13. Artificial Intelligence and Machine Learning Solutions
- 14. Voice-over Solutions
- 15. Automated Marketing Solutions
- 16. Customized Travel Experiences
- 17. Seasonal & Holiday Themed Products
- 18. Augmented Reality Solutions
- 19. IOT Solutions
- 20. Auto Follow Drones and Underwater Drones

Chapter 4

HOW TO VALIDATE A BUSINESS IDEA THROUGH FEEDBACK?

Most first-time entrepreneurs skip the feedback process because admittedly it's not only a boring thing to do but it requires stepping out of your comfort zone and people don't want to do it as much as they have to do it. But it's absolutely wise and necessary to get help. You cannot do everything on your own. Getting feedback is a part of your planning process. It helps you to determine if your idea is good. Others can help you see perspectives that you cannot see.

> *"Only the paranoid survive."*
> *– Andy Grove, former CEO of Intel*

After we complete the section on getting feedback and advice we're going to get into how to think strategically about your business which can help you to reason with it independently while at the same time getting other's perspectives. Bringing the best of both worlds will set you a very strong foundation to start your business.

Tool 6: Validate your Business Idea

So, with that, let's get started. So, you've got a business niche, a business idea. How do you know if it's any good? You've got to get feedback. It's an absolute must. You can't get around that. Writing from experience I know that it's actually not easy to get feedback and sometimes there's an impulse to skip it entirely because often you don't want to hear bad feedback. Really, it's not that easy at times to get valuable feedback and it's just process that you know little of. Did I get enough feedback? Is it right? Who knows right?

When I was doing it for my ideas I was consistently making the mistake of not getting enough feedback, getting into businesses without enough support or advice. I made plenty of mistakes here before. So, let's discuss how you should go about looking for feedback and from whom we should get it and after that, I'll show you some techniques.

Image by Clker from Pixabay

First of all, the easiest option you have is to consult your friends and family. They'll always discuss with you (hopefully). But the problem is that they lack objectivity. They're afraid for you to get hurt and they might be worried for you to get into the business. Almost all the time they might be good at business but maybe not the one that you're starting. So, are family really the deep level experts like the kinds you need? Nope.

All right, so to get good feedback you have to start looking beyond the family. Don't get me wrong, sometimes you may get an honest perspective but it's not the complete picture, right? So, then you move on to the next layer, which is your business peers. That's the next level of feedback you need essentially. You start with your acquaintances and maybe friends. Then you take the next step and venture out of the building and go to networking events wherever you live. If you don't know where to find the networking events, just use Google, Facebook, Meetup, or any other event listing. You could join some networking groups in your area but do remember that most groups often have a membership fee. I personally am part of several networking groups like TIE.

So, we have learnt that it is good to expand your network beyond family and friends. You have to reach out and find networking and business networking events wherever you live. If your idea is pertaining to a specific industry, let's say you are getting into mobile apps, then you just type 'mobile app events' or 'mobile app business networking' in your city and you'll find plenty of options. Like I said, reach out. You never know when you end up being in the right place at the right time. Simple, just find events that matter to you and your industry, where you can go, network and discuss with people. Such events are generally accessible and you find a whole bunch of peers there.

So now we have moved from family, friends and acquaintances to networking with business peers. The problem is they also lack deep insight. So, you have to go further from where you can get meaningful insights. Well, nobody can give you a better insight than your customers. They know what they like and what works or doesn't work for them. So, the next step is to identify who your customers might be.

And of course, you might say well everybody can be my customer. Yes, but who is the ideal person you're thinking of when you're creating your business or service. Discuss with those people, seek them out. It's not easy but this is the theory of customer development methodology by Steve Blank (www.steveblank.com). He is an extremely respected business person and a Stanford Business School professor. The idea behind this is essentially getting out of your comfort zone. Go discuss with your potential customers and with people you think could be your customers. Most of them are not going to discuss with you. So, you're going to have some rejection. But, some of them will discuss with you and they will give you insights. So, this is a must, to know and find your potential customer. Just remember to structure that conversation properly. Later, in this chapter, I will go through this structure in detail.

So when you do get into a discussion with your potential customers, remember these few tips. Listen more talk less. Tell them the idea. But listen to their feedback and really take it in and think about it. You don't have to follow their feedback and take their advice but certainly, think about it a lot. If they give you positive feedback, ask them something like "Would you buy this?" and see where that conversation goes. If they say 'yeah!' well, then you have your first customer signed up almost before your business even launched because you can then come back to them. So that's potential customers. Get out of your comfort zone, find those potential customers and ask hard questions. It's usually more enlightening than people think it will be. And some people skip this process and then it comes back to bite them. So, do not skip this process.

And then, of course, there are industry experts. People who are the most knowledgeable in that specific industry, who are not potential clients. How do you find them? Traditionally, it's really hard to find them because they're obviously extremely busy and a lot of people want their time and want to get their advice. So how do you actually get their advice? Well in almost any industry, what I do is I go to Facebook groups and LinkedIn groups that are professional groups and I find potential groups where people are networking. Let me tell you just how simple that would be.

Let's say you have an idea for a podcast and you want to get feedback on it. It can be anything. It can be a new widget, anything, but let's say that podcasting is your thing. All you do is you search for something like podcasting group on Facebook. You can do the same thing on LinkedIn and look for groups that you can join. And look at how many people there are. Benchmark would be 5000 -15000. And you start engaging there. Just don't post super beginner questions and don't post promotional questions of anything you're promoting. Try to ask interesting questions and see who helps you and see whose answers are the most helpful. Then you can sort of start privately chatting with them and get more help. And then what might happen is that you start to benefit the moment you start forming some basic relationships with the people in these forums.

Yes, it's true that experts answer there but remember there's a lot of beginners too and the problem is people cannot say a lot of things publicly. There are just some things you have to be professional about. In every industry, there are some unspoken elements and rules. Those topics are usually spoken about in private groups. So, with whoever you form relationships with, ask them, "hey are you a member of any private groups about podcasting?" (yes, I am still with that example). And most of the time they'll say no but in case somebody ever says yes, it will be 10 levels more eye-opening than just being in a group like this.

And I know this from experience because those groups are typically invite-only and they have more earnest and honest discussions. But even if you don't join those, some people who reply to you in the basic groups might be extremely successful and feedback from them would be of utmost value. If you want private feedback from them you might have to pay some money for their coaching (if they even offer that). But in a group like this, they might just be open to helping you out with a little bit of advice just because that's what the theme of the group is – everybody helps each other.

> *"Don't let others convince you that the idea is good when your gut tells you it's bad."*
>
> *– Kevin Rose, co-founded Digg*

So, this is how you find all kinds of different people to give you feedback on your ideas.

Now let's discuss a few paid or very difficult places to get feedback. First, let's discuss the paid options, these involve hiring coaches and hiring experts. What you would want to look for in a coach or expert is deep expertise in specifically the area that you are starting your business in. The first place to go is something called Clarity.fm. This is a place where you can hire experts and pay them to get on a phone call with you. Other options are freelancing sites like fiverr.com or upwork.com where there are a lot of the experts. There are a lot of the freelancers who might have some expertise in your field and instead of actually hiring them directly for their work maybe you hire them for 30 minutes or an hour or two hours just to discuss with them and get their feedback. It costs a little bit but you might find people who will be readily available for you just because you're paying them and it's not that much at the end of the day. Also, you can search Google for mastermind groups for subject area of your idea and see if you can find any. Usually, you can find some and if you don't, just ask around in social media and people might point you in the right direction.

To look beyond the paid options, we have to now consider the most difficult but the most rewarding feedback. This is feedback from Mentors. This option is usually free but hard to find. To find the right mentors is tough, but even tougher is to get to work with them because you need to build a relationship with them first. Good mentors are great experts typically, and that means they have a lot of people bugging them and asking them for help and advice. So, what that means for you is you have to stand out and they have to be interested in devoting their time with you so that's going to be a little difficult. Difficult, but rewarding.

Usually, you have to be self-driven and motivated. Not someone who says I'm motivated and then doesn't do anything. You have to be someone, who can take an inch and go a mile with that. They give you a tiny bit of advice. You take that, you run with it. You do something with it. You show them results. And that's how you build that mentor relationship. They will like you because they get rewarded if you do hit success, as experienced business people like to help new business people.

But the problem with the new business people is they just take and don't give back. If it's not rewarding for the mentor, then they shun you early. So, as long as you're a go-getter and self-driven, independent and consistent, you definitely will go further and further. It's actually intellectually stimulating for a lot of experienced business people to be helping you. And they get a kick out of it because they feel rewarded as they're helping you. So that's how you can position yourself to be more likely to get a mentor. But even if you don't, there are some paid options for how to get a lot of great feedback.

> *"If we tried to think of a good idea, we wouldn't have been able to think of a good idea. You just have to find the solution for a problem in your own life."*
>
> *– Brian Cheeky, Co-founder of Airbnb*

Now let's discuss how to structure your conversation in which you get your business idea feedback. You have to do two things:

HOW TO VALIDATE A BUSINESS IDEA THROUGH FEEDBACK?

a. Treat it like a meeting.

b. Be grateful no matter if they are mean to you.

If they're not helpful even if you're paying them, you still have to carry yourself with a certain degree of professionalism. If you are paying for it and you see early that it's not helping you then you want to cut that short because you're paying for it.

So how do you treat it like a meeting?

First of all, you have to ask that person how much time they have from 5 minutes to 15 minutes to 30 minutes to an hour. These are all tremendously different conversations for the amount of time that you have. You need to fit your most burning questions into that because you have to set your goals. You've got to set the goals like, "I need to get at least that question answered" or "at least that problem solved", so that you can come back with a solution. If you just go ask a million questions and they are not in a sequence or organized, you would distract the person giving feedback with your unfocused approach. This would waste a ton of time and not get you anywhere. Another tip is to take notes if possible. I learnt this very early. These days I tag team. I actually also take notes at the end of every meeting to catch the essence of it. No point moving on to the next meeting till you have captured all the feedback in your notes. And if it's more of a formal situation where you're really getting the feedback, ask them if you can record it so that you can come back to that later. If not, just take notes, preferable right after the end of the discussion after they leave, on your phone, pad or on paper.

Make sure that you have your quick and clear pitch ready when you start a conversation so that you can tell them what you're doing. I often run into would be entrepreneurs with no clarity of concept. They go on and on explaining their idea and how good it is. So please be clear in your mind and words. If you cannot explain your idea, problem, solution and value proposition in one line (max two) then you are not clear. Period. Work on that. After your initial pitch and explanation of 1-2 lines, ask them your first question. It could be about what you need help with. From there on, you listen more than debate or discuss. Don't start defending your idea, listen and absorb the feedback.

Feedback can sometimes be negative. Don't argue, do not get defensive, do not start finding excuses and wish your problems away. Like I said, sit there listen and absorb. Don't react adversely. So what if they're giving you negative feedback? Take it as if you were giving a presentation. Not everyone has to like what they see and hear. Don't judge people because they have a different opinion. Consider the points they have made and use it to better your proposition. Feedback also allows you to improve your pitch. Every pitch you make, you tweak it a little with every feedback.

Usually, if you ask them questions then you must have follow up questions, right? So if you have multiple conversations like this you probably get similar answers to some questions in the beginning. And after a while you start skipping some questions and you end up with questions that are unanswered. So just make sure that you have asked your follow-up questions. The trick is to be ready for the meeting and try to stay away from questions that give obvious or generic answers because then you'll get exactly that. The way to understand this better is Close-ended and Open-ended questions. Close-ended questions should be used in surveys while open-ended questions should be used in interviews for feedback.

Also, remember to not be too generic in your questions. It's kind of like people just sometimes fall back on the boring answer that they give to everybody just because it's there and they don't have to think too hard. So, don't ask something like "How do you start a business?" Instead, ask something specific like "How do I go about registration?" or "Do you know how to find that particular something?" Ask specific things that you can't Google by yourself and that they might have a true insight to. That's a good barometer.

I came up with a small list of questions that I get asked that I dislike the most because I discuss with a lot of people and some questions come up all the time. So, my all time disliked questions are:

How much money can I make?

This is perhaps tied for my least favourite. I don't like this question. Because my answer is always like you know it depends on you hundred percent. Of course, you can make money but most people don't because they don't execute well. You haven't started and are getting too greedy too soon. Focus on being good first. Money comes later. That's usually how I think about it.

Can you give me a good business idea?

This is another question which comes up when sometimes people give me an idea and that's not so great. And the moment I give my first feedback they jump to "Can you give me a good business idea?" Well, I don't know that person. I can tell them that go build the next Google. That's a fantastic business idea. But can they build that? So, I don't know what would they like to do. I know I can tell them Go to YouTube, Go to Amazon. I don't know if they want to do that. How can I give somebody ideas when I don't even know them?

So, brainstorm and think don't just ask for ready-made things, learn to think on your feet. Learn to be better. So, the questions I would have preferred to hear is *"How can I execute well?"* and follow up questions as well should be like *"What does it take to execute well?"* like *"how do I do this? how do I do this tactic? how to implement that?"*, something that shows you've thought of it or you tried it yourself, not as if you're just a daydreamer. Those are the kinds of questions that I'd like to be asked. They are more interesting for me to answer.

More on questions: Let's say you are looking for people who go 'Wow!' when tell them your idea and provide you with the validation you need. Even if you have managed to evoke a reaction. So sometimes a technique entrepreneurs use is, if you're discussing to potential clients and the clients say yeah I like it, then the next set of questions would lead to asking OK if you like it that much, would you sign up to buy now ahead of time? I'll give you a discount or something like that. It's not a possible thing to suggest in all cases but often you just basically test how true is it.

Now let's discuss cheaply testing your business ideas because as you go through your process of getting theoretical feedback from friends, family, business peers, potential customers, from experts, from mentors, one thing you have to remember is to do it all at the bare minimum cost. Now let's discuss how to start testing your idea in a practical sense because it's better to build the business earlier rather than later. So you can start testing, start learning, start small. Remember, to make it affordable and economical. No one wants failure but I would rather have a cheap failure. Everybody wants to succeed but for me a cheap failure is much better than sitting on the side-lines for too long, not failing but also not starting. You want to fail cheaply and learn by doing and not just sit there and theoretically wonder.

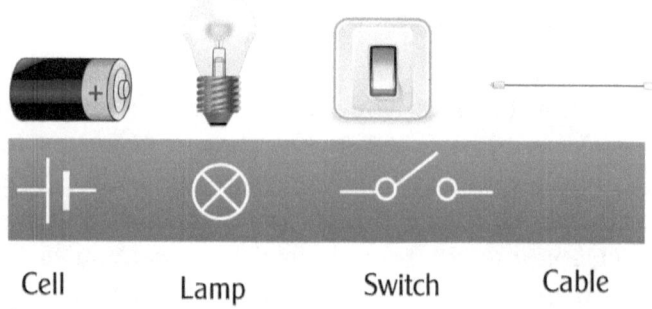

Image by Oberholster Venita from Pixabay

Tool 7: *Minimum Viable Product - MVP*

So for this purpose, let me introduce the concept of MVP, which stands for Minimum Viable Product. It's a very basic product to start with, so that it's cheap to create. You can launch it and start getting feedback rather than overbuild something that's going to be much more costly. Because, you don't even know if those features that you had planned are going to be features that your users like or whether you can even get users for your product. Right.

So, before you dive in let's go over a few questions that you should ask yourself just kind of a last sanity checks before you dive in and start testing cheaply. Can you really pull it off? I mean, you might have a good business idea, sure, but can you do it? Does it require some specific skills that you don't have in-house? Does it require resources like a lot of money, man-hours, some inventory or tools? Sometimes we come up with expensive to execute ideas that just cost a lot of money. We get fake inspiration from disruptive models and think if I throw a lot of money at it, I will be able to capture the market. But, how are you going to get that money? How are you going to raise that kind of dough? It's not that easy to raise money. Sometimes it's a question like, "are you entering an interesting business space?" Let me give an example: let's say you wanted to get into the newspaper industry. Well, you better have a really good reason now because that industry is in decline. So, think about what ecosystem are you entering. Because on the flip side of the newspaper industry which is not a popular one today, there is another industry that might be very popular today.

Another example: many people get into mobile app games. So many people build gaming apps. Everyone wants to get into that as it's really fun. It's awesome to have people playing your app but it's unbelievably difficult to succeed because there are hundreds of thousands maybe millions of games out there and most of them fail. So, it's a wildly competitive space. So, think about the ecosystem because you'll have to face the challenges of whatever ecosystem you're entering.

You just want to make sure that those are reasonable challenges, not ones that are too difficult to overcome. So, let's discuss now how to do some real-world testing for your ideas cheaply. I will try to take a few different examples which might not apply to all businesses but would be helpful for many of you. If you are selling products, let's say you want to design clothing T-shirts or you want to sell physical products maybe on Amazon or on Shopify site, you definitely want to start with a small amount of inventory, no bulk buying as the bulk buying will be too much risk. The smaller inventory will be just to test whether you are able to sell and if the product is accepted by the market. If you are able to sell the small set of inventories even if it was a little bit costly to acquire, it still makes financial sense. We are always trying to test and minimize the bigger risk. Because the reality is that most people don't sell. And so, they end up being stuck with this inventory. If you want to sell online then put up a basic Website and start basic promotion of the site to see how it goes. Also, if you need to shoot videos or click pictures, like some people, you can either wait for a long time to get great equipment like an amazing camera, lighting, studio and so on. Or you can also figure out how to film from your phone which has an HD camera or the webcam of your laptop for free with reasonably good sound quality on your own. You may invest in budget-friendly equipment that might cost you under a hundred dollars and start getting feedback.

> *"Play by the rules, but be ferocious."*
>
> *– Phil Knight*

If you feel that all these tests are going to take a while, you can start quickly too. For example, let's say you have an online idea that's hard to promote. Probably there's some Website that makes it easy for you. For example, if you wanted to do your own Shopify store you can even start selling on Amazon before you set up your Shopify site. If you want to have some agency business like a marketing agency, it would be worthwhile to become a freelancer first. It's much easier to start that way and at least you get your feet wet and start learning sooner rather than later because that's the goal.

A lot of the assumptions that you have while you're sitting there theoretically dreaming about the business, they all go away after you start and you learn the reality of that business. So don't procrastinate. Start smart by having a MVP and test your idea in the real-world by launching something quickly.

> *"You have to see failure as the beginning and the middle, but never entertain it as an end."*
>
> *– Jessica Herrin, founder and CEO of Stella & Dot*

Some Customer Feedback Questions You Could Ask Your Customers

- How would you describe yourself in one sentence?
- What is your main goal for using this website/product?
- What, if anything, is preventing you from achieving that goal?
- What is your greatest concern about (product/brand)?
- What changed for you after you started using our product?
- Where did you first hear about us?
- Have you used our [product or service) before?
- Why did you choose to use our [product or service) over other options?
- Have you used a similar (product or service) before?
- How do you use our product/service?
- How can we make this page better?

- What's the ONE thing our website is missing?
- What, if anything, is stopping you from (taking action) today?
- What are your main concerns or questions about (product or service)?
- Thanks for (taking action)! How are you planning to use (product or service)?
- How would you describe the buying experience?
- Do you feel our (product or service) is worth the cost?
- What convinced you to buy the product?
- What challenges are you trying to solve?
- What nearly stopped you from buying?
- What do you like most about our (product or service)?
- What do you like least?
- What feature/option could we add to make your experience better?
- How could we have gone above and beyond?
- Net Promoter Score (NPS) how likely are you to recommend our products?
- Customer Satisfaction (CSAT) how satisfied are you with our product/services?
- Customer Effort Score (CES) how easy did (organization) make it for you to solve your issue?
- Is there anything you'd like to add?

Chapter 5

BUSINESS PLAN

More often than not the factor that determines the fate of any business or start-up idea is not the idea itself, but rather the action plan or the business plan. Any entrepreneurial venture starts with an idea. What sustains that idea all the way through is the business plan. It helps in maintaining focus and getting from the point of incubation to the vision one might have for their start-up. A plan acts as a step-by-step guide to achieve the vision for any business while keeping the goals realistic and achievable. It helps in achieving the short-term objectives that would help achieve the long-term objective. An awesome idea might see itself fail because the execution and overall vision for the idea had not been thoroughly thought through. While at the same time an idea that is not quite that revolutionary might see itself bloom into a successful venture because the execution and the plan to see the idea through was well laid out.

It is like Benjamin Franklin said, *"If you fail to plan, you are planning to fail."*

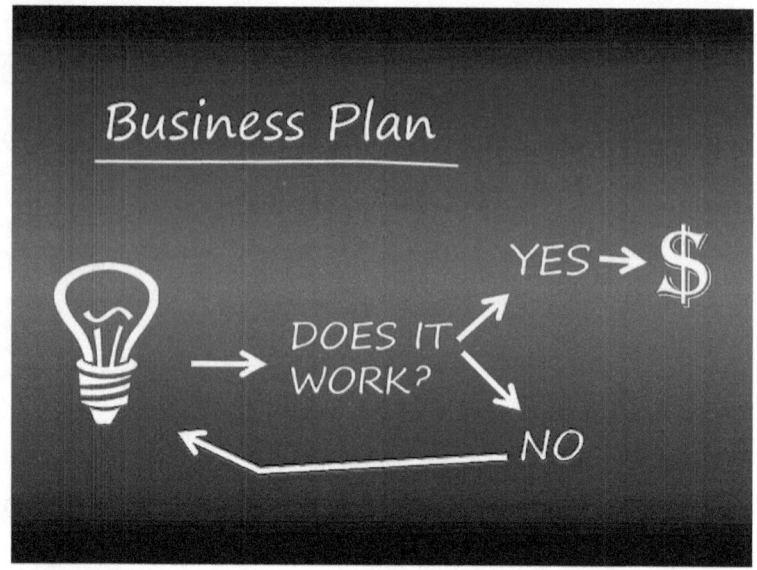

Image by Openclipart from Pixabay

To help you in the process of making a business idea I have compiled my experience into this chapter and will give you an awesome hack later. This would give you a holistic view of the art of making a business plan and seeing them all the way through.

Let us start by familiarizing ourselves with business plans by looking at some examples and the templates generally followed in the process of making business plans. There is some information that is a must-have in any business plan. Executive summary, product summary, market summary and financial projections. An executive summary is a basic summary of the idea. It is better to pair it up with what you imagine is the key to the success of your business and it could be topped off by some quote or saying to give weight to the whole thing. The plan should also include a company summary, telling what the company and its people are, followed by the product summary which talks about the services and products provided by the company. A product summary should then be followed by a Market Summary that deals with the market for the product and the competition that is present in the market. It is also important to keep the summaries concise. It is just a lot of good information that you need to whittle down so that it does not overwhelm the board or the people you were giving this to at the time. The Plan is also needed to gather funds for the project and thus should be clear and concise as it has to be presented to many persons of interest. A profit and loss projection for the next 12 months is also recommended to be added to the plan.

Tool 8: Starting the Business Plan

But to start the writing of the plan, it is very important to understand your company by visualizing the entire system and then putting down the most important aspects. To create a business plan summary, the three main questions you should ask about your business and product:

- Who?
- What?
- How?

    - **Who?**

        The "Who" is your customer. The most important aspect and this is exactly where you should start. Who is your basic understanding of *"Who is your Client?"* and *"Who will be buying your product or service?"*. This should be followed by your clear understanding and putting down the answers about the clients/customers you have written above. These questions are: *"Where do I sell to these customers?* and *"How do I reach them?"*. Finally, you need to go a little bit deeper and write the answers to *"How will I be managing my relationship and sales with these customers-sales and after-sales?"*

- **What?**

    The "What" is your Offer. What is your Value proposition? In the what part you should be able to answer clearly *"What is the value that my product/service generate for the customer I identified?"* followed by, *"Why should the customer be paying for my product/service?"* and *"What is the benefit I am able to provide to my prospective clients?"*

- **How?**

    The "How" is your infrastructure. You start by getting a grasp of and writing down the answer to *"what are all my key and essential resources?"* Then comes the understanding of your key activities. *"What are the activities I need to conduct to bring that value mentioned above to my customers?"* While you are at it, jot down *"what are the key partnerships you can form?* and equally important *"who could I collaborate with to execute?* And, *"what part of all the activities do I need to delegate and to whom?"*

UNDERSTAND THE FINANCES:

After answering the "Who", "What", and "How", you have to be able to answer the questions about your finances and your revenue model. Answer the following and you will understand the finances to start with. *"How do I make revenue/money?"* *"How much can I charge for my product/service?"* and finally, *"What is it going to cost me to do all this?"* Revenue and cost need to be understood before we start that venture.

So now we have got everything we need to start with writing a perfect business plan. I can't emphasize enough the importance of business planning. Many entrepreneurs are not aware of the importance of business planning and some believe that a business plan is something that is hardly required. I can tell you with experience that you need to put together an efficient business plan cause that is your introduction when the company needs a bank loan or is seeking outside equity capital.

THE BUSINESS PLAN FORMAT:

The format provides you with a framework for presenting your thoughts, ideas and strategies in a logical, consistent and coherent manner. In other words, the business plan format helps you to clarify your ideas and present them clearly to others.

1. Executive Summary
2. Enterprise Description
3. Product or Service Description
4. Industry Analysis
5. Competition Analysis
6. Swot Analysis
7. Marketing Sub-Plan
8. Operations Sub-Plan
9. Human Resources Sub-Plan
10. The Budget
11. Liquidity
12. Financial Sub-Plan
13. Selected Options and Critical Measures
14. Milestone Schedule

Tool 9: The practical Business Plan

We have all the ingredients already to write this business plan as we took a systematic approach in understanding our business first. But this is what you can google, so where does my expertise come in? Well, I have written or seen up to hundreds. If not thousands, of business plans and at this point, I've developed a system to streamline the entire process not only making it faster and simpler but also way more useful in a really practical way.

So in my hack, the business plan has only 7 main sections, namely:

1. Executive Summary
2. Product/Service Analysis
3. Customer Analysis
4. Offer & Value Proposition
5. SWOT Analysis
6. Marketing Plan
7. Financial Plan

I believe having a business plan with these sections could really give insights and help the start-ups in making it to the other side.

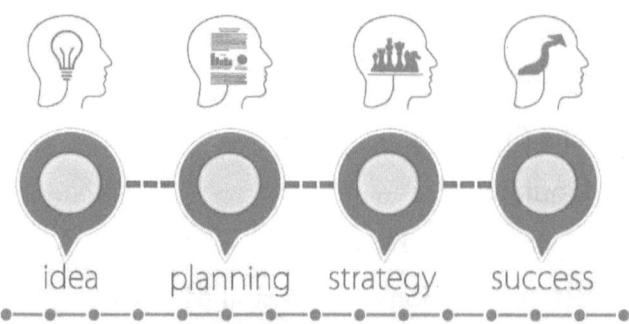

Image by Gerd Altmann from Pixabay

1. **Executive Summary:**

    I must highlight the significance of brainstorming and rewarding good ideas. I want to ask would-be entrepreneurs to explore the market and do comparative research with their competition. The significance of an executive summary cannot be ignored. If you are pitching your business plan to venture capitalists, a bank, or potential investors you want to make sure that your executive summary captures their attention and gives them the motivation to read on beyond the first page. The purpose of your executive summary is to quickly and briefly summarize the details of the sections of the business plan. The potential investor should be enticed to read the next step. Talking about identifying your target consumer base, if you cannot identify who is going to buy your product or services how can you expect banks and investors to loan you money to sell to somebody you don't even know exists or can properly identify. That is why we had started with the answer to "Who?"

Listing your top-level employees along with their experiences can be another attraction point to the investors. Discussing the optimum length of the Executive summary and Business plan I must add that think of your executive summary as the halfway point between your elevator pitch and your business plan. So the main sections of a perfect Executive Summary are:

- The Idea
- The Problem
- The Solution
- The Opportunity
- Your Competitive Advantage
- The Business Model
- The Team
- The Vision and Promise

2. **Product/Service Analysis**

   The first task in product/service analysis is to become familiar with and understand your product/service. You have to answer a few questions for your product/service to be analyzed. So I would like to give you some points to get you started.

   - What does it do?
   - How does it do it?
   - What does it look like?
   - Identify your market potential
   - Estimate your price
   - Forecast your sales volume
   - Identify your break-even point

3. **Customer Analysis**

   Remember we started with understanding the "Who". A customer analysis, profile or persona is a critical section of your business plan. It identifies target customers, ascertains the needs of these customers, and then specifies how your product or service satisfies these needs. While you are writing your customer profile, do look into behavior and demographics. Ask yourself two follow-up questions *"Why does your product match a customer's lifestyle"* and *"What is the customer's age, race, ethnicity, gender, marital status, income, education, and employment?"*

   A customer analysis is a simple tool that can help you better understand potential customers, so you could increase sales and grow your business. Customer profiles are a collection of information about customers that help determine why people buy or won't buy a product. Customer analysis can also help develop specific marketing plans and ensure that products or services address the needs of the intended audience.

4. **Offer & Value Proposition**

   You have to know and be able to communicate your value proposition. Preconceptions can have a huge negative impact on your business plan. Do not assume that anyone who will be reading your business plan knows anything about your business. You will need to include a number of specific pieces of information that will help the reader to understand exactly how you have set up the business.

   Creating a value proposition is the integral part of a business and its strategy. This strategy is based on finding a value proposition for your customer. Value can be created and sustained only if you have a satisfied customer.

   So, what makes a value proposition? You have to analyze the benefits, costs, and value that you can deliver to your potential customers.

5. **SWOT Analysis**

   SWOT analysis can also be used to add a certain zing factor to your plan. Preparing a concise and attractive SWOT might be the key to getting investors interested in your venture.

   SWOT stands for

   - Strengths
   - Weaknesses
   - Opportunities
   - Threats

     SWOT Analysis is a technique for assessing these four aspects of your business.

You can use SWOT Analysis to make the most of what you've got and understand your company's foremost advantages. You would be able to reduce the chances of failure, understand what you're missing, and eliminate dangers. Being aware is the key.

So, SWOT would help you not only understand but better still, craft a strategy that differentiates you from your competitors, so you could compete in the market, successfully.

6. **Marketing Plan**

Marketing plans are all about identifying your target market and customers and then creating suitable strategies for reaching those customers. You have to incorporate sales plans and detail the strategies the business will use to sell products or services to increase revenue. The sales plan often forms part of the marketing strategy.

Your business marketing plan is a blueprint for reaching your customer base. We will study the customer journey blueprint later on in this book. The first step in developing a marketing plan is to consider clearly who your target customers are. Ask yourself who your main customers are, what they are looking for and what you need to do to be able to provide what this customer wants.

Marketing plans must incorporate goal setting. Goal setting for an entrepreneur is an important task because it holds you accountable for the tasks that will eventually increase your profit margins, help you gain new traction and customers. It is not an easy task to be working on marketing plans and strategies, so, setting goals can help keep you within a timeline that is both challenging and rewarding.

No matter the content or the format of your marketing plan, you can't ignore the fact that marketing and promotion strategies are important for the long-term viability of your business. We now live in a world that is interconnected and definitely, the competition runs very high. The marketing plans can help you stand-out among your competitors by connecting with your customers with time-tested strategies and particularly in new, innovative ways.

7. **Financial Plan**

    Most upcoming entrepreneurs have trouble in the financial section. It's one of the most intensive and intimidating parts of the business plan. So I want to make it easy to understand by talking about the basics of creating financials for your business plan. The Profit and Loss Projection and Cash Flow statement are the must-haves in the financials of business plans. You must cover all kinds of expenses in your financial plan, including the insurances, the interest on loans, the marketing and modelling expense, the salaries and wages of all kinds of employees and so on.

    Put in a little bit more effort when it comes to the finances. I would like to give you a six-step approach to getting financial summaries and financial plan. The six steps are:

    1. Start-up Expenses
    2. Start-up Assets
    3. Monthly Expenses
    4. Finance Options
    5. Revenue Projections
    6. Profit and Loss

So there you have it. A 7-step hack/tool to a perfect business plan.

Now let's talk about the three most important steps that an entrepreneur must follow to grow his idea into a successful venture. The first and most important thing is the passion and love behind an idea. An entrepreneur must truly love and believe in his idea and should not be in the business simply to make money. You have to ask yourself whether you love your business idea enough to persist with it and keep going with it to eventually turn it into something successful. The second step is value generation. You must know the market well enough to generate value for your consumers. The third step is to start your business with a minimum viable model until it can sustain itself or you have built it into a model that would self-sustain eventually.

Along with these three points, planning is one of the most critical business functions. Success is very difficult to achieve without proper planning. With the help of the information I have given you, you would be able to create a business plan document. This would save money for your business in several ways. You have to make the effort to seek out these savings. A rigorous planning process can also help you uncover exciting new revenue opportunities in the coming times.

I hate to tell you but great ideas are totally useless if you cannot formulate and execute a plan that separates success and failure. I give particular importance to the cash flow statement. The cash flow statement is the most important because it takes into account your monthly expenses and basically all the money coming into and going out of your business and when that happens. I must also acknowledge the importance of an executive summary, but let's take an unorthodox approach to it. VCs and investors basically only read the executive summary and the financial statements in the back so you better make sure that this is a really good summary of you and your business plan. Tradition says that it should be one page. I say with an executive summary you want to go into as much detail as you can. You want to hit them with all the highlights but you know do it succinctly and briefly.

The idea and timing are very important. The essence of all of this is, as I would say, in summary, execution definitely matters a lot. So to conclude, let's talk about the ideal business plan. Don't have a plan that is just based on money. Money should be the consequence of success and not success in itself. Have a positive attitude and a positive mental state. A decision-maker can often perceive a situation to be different than what it actually is and make mistakes. Think of a long-term plan. So let me conclude by giving a road map and the following pointers: -

- Do Good Things, give back to society.
- Accountability, your plan, your responsibility.
- Timeframe, think long term.
- Leadership, with integrity.

With the technicalities in mind and a decent template, focus on the important stuff and with a positive mental outlook, you too can make a business plan that would be the roadmap that leads your idea to become a successful business.

> *"Success is not final; failure is not fatal: it is the courage to continue that counts."*
>
> *– Winston Churchill*

PROBLEM	SOLUTION	UNIQUE VALUE PROPOSITION	UNFAIR ADVANTAGE	CUSTOMER SEGMENTS
List your top 3 problems.	Outline a possible solution for each problem.	Single, clear, compelling message that states why you are different and worth paying attention.	Something that cannot easily be bought or copied.	List your target customers and users.
	KEY METRICS	HIGH-LEVEL CONCEPT	CHANNELS	EARLY ADOPTERS
EXISTING ALTERNATIVES	List the key numbers that tell you how your business is doing.	List your X or Y analogy e.g. YouTube Flickr for videos.	List your path to customers (inbound or outbound).	List the characteristics of your ideal customers.
List how these problems are solved today		CHANNELS		
		List your path to customers (inbound or outbound).		
COST STRUCTURE			REVENUE STREAMS	
List your fixed and variable costs.			List your sources of revenue.	

Lean Canvas is adapted from The Business Model Canvas and is licensed under the Creative Commons Attribution–Share Alike 3.0 Unported License.

Chapter 6

BUSINESS RISKS YOU MUST BE AWARE OF

> "The reason so many people fail to achieve their goals is because they have not committed to defending a time in which they will work on their goals."
>
> – Steve McClatchy

Image by Wokandapix from Pixabay

Most people know that business can be risky but most people don't distinguish between the types of risk. Of course, most people, when they talk about a business being risky, they are normally referring to the financial risk. Everyone does understand that if things don't go right, there is a probability of losing your money. It's a known thing. It is also a known fact that many businesses fail. It's especially risky if you take a loan or use money that is not yours to start a business. After that, you have to also consider things like the time that you're spending working on your business. Maybe that's the money that you're not earning from a job you could have been doing. So, there's a lot of different ways to calculate risk. When you start your company, the risk is one thing that you need to try and minimize. I had discussed earlier that you need to start small, especially if you're a first-time entrepreneur because most first-time entrepreneurs make a lot of costly mistakes. And ideally, you want to learn cheaply. So be careful of high costs when starting out and always try to see whether you could do something more economically. By now, you would be wondering about other types of risks out there. Well, I did mention financial and time linked to opportunity risk. There's another kind of risk called product risk. This is something that applies to complicated products. Let's say you have some interesting new start-up idea but it takes a lot of programming hours and you have to pay for the programming hours and you have to outsource the work or maybe it's going to take many months.

Basically, I want to share with you the five top reasons I see entrepreneurs or their businesses fail and I've been observing this over the years with thousands of entrepreneurs. So this is a very accurate list and I really hope that you take this to heart and think about it and see where you are when it comes to risk and see what kind of pitfalls you might be falling into right now.

BUSINESS RISKS YOU MUST BE AWARE OF

> *"When you take risks and they work out, they lead to new capabilities you never saw before."*
> – Tom Soderstrom

Tool 10: Understand Risk and Save money

So, let's talk about the five types of business risk that are there typically and then I shall segregate based on which risk is okay and which ones you want to minimize.

RISK 1: WAITING TOO LONG TO START

The first one is actually not starting at all or waiting too long to start. Delay in starting can be due to various reasons, maybe you are waiting to get some money, maybe you're waiting till you can free up some time, maybe you don't have an office. It might be a maybe something else or you would have found an excuse to convince yourself to procrastinate. What would entrepreneurs do? They start. They make things work. They find the way where non-entrepreneurs find excuses. If you're waiting too long like even over two to three months, you're making the absolute number one mistake of entrepreneurship. No matter what you do, just start doing it. Stop sitting around and just find the way. Don't waste too much money but find a way to do it cheaply.

RISK 2: NOT BEING CONSISTENT

The second mistake is not putting in a consistent long-term effort. This is a direct risk to your chances of being successful. When you start you are sure to pump, huff and puff for a week or 2-3 months. You might have great momentum in the beginning, but to build a business you need consistent work over many months or years. Every day or nearly every day and with intensity. If you were practicing a musical instrument you would ask me how much should I practice. I would say as much as possible and consistently. Well, this is exactly the same. You need to be working how you would practice, nearly every day and as intensely and consistently as possible. Put in the hours and the results will come. Entrepreneurship is an art form, like a musical instrument, that can be learnt, but you need to be practicing hard and as much as you can.

RISK 3: NOT GROWING YOUR CRAFT

Mistake number three is not growing beyond your main craft. In these times day and age, this is a huge risk. We have to be learning and evolving. Let's say you're great at cooking. You want to open a restaurant. Fantastic. But you need to learn management, you need to learn marketing, you need to learn to raise funds. All those additional skills, you've got to learn them. Yes, you would be still a great cook, but others would take advantage of your lack of basic knowledge in other domains. This would eventually lead to failure or you would end up paying through your nose just to stay relevant and afloat. You don't have to learn every possible skill in your business, but you have to grow beyond your skillset and pick up new skills especially early on. Every business needs an understanding of basic core skills that your business needs, so you need to learn them. We normally feel that we would be able to outsource every other resource, but that in itself is a recipe for disaster. You can't outsource too much too fast. You have got to learn a lot of skills.

Enough about skills you might at this stage feel are irrelevant for you. Even then you have to keep evolving. Let's stick with the example of cooking. You are great at it. But times change and along with it the preferences of people you cook for. People would want vegan, keto or any other preferential food that you might not be cooking. So, if you are not constantly growing your craft and adding to your menu dishes catering to the need of the times, you are bound to falter eventually.

Risk 4: Not having a Marketing Strategy

Most entrepreneurs when they start their marketing strategy, no matter their business, use an identical approach. They promote their business with flyers and then think they have hit jackpot by marketing and giving ads on social media platforms like Facebook and Instagram. Everyone thinks of referrals, hopefully. Well if that's your marketing strategy that's not quite a marketing strategy. That's just the first thing that comes to mind for most people. You've got to dig in there. That's a sign that you might be falling into that pitfall because your marketing strategy has to be specifically curated for the kind of situation and business you have. A customized marketing strategy is a must. Expand your thought horizon and really think. The key to the puzzle is understanding your customer. I will cover this aspect in the coming chapters. You need to understand your customer and the journey they take with you at every point of interaction you might have, to be able to nail the marketing strategy. I make comics to attract customers to my education platform, www.leapwaters.com. It can be as vague or unique. Think.

Risk 5: Mismatch of the Founder

Ideas are good. Ideas can be great. But just because you had an awesome idea does not mean you could execute it. This is the meaning of mismatch of the founder to the business. Like a lot of people come to me, they haven't done much work on the web and they come to me and they're like I want to make online passive income. Well yeah. Every person online would want to be or trying to do that. It's even hard for people good at it, and for someone, with no particular experience, it is going to be even harder. So, you really have to draw on your skills for the business that you're starting. And if you're starting from scratch it's absolutely okay. But you should realize that your first three to six months are going to be a complete learning curve. You are very likely not going to succeed and would probably just be going through the mistakes and learning from them.

So, these are the top five risks that are out there and the top five mistakes entrepreneurs make. So please do consider these risks with seriousness. Avoid them and you would have carved a much better way for yourself to be successful.

MORE MISTAKES THAT ENTREPRENEURS MAKE:

The discussion and the topic of risks does not end there. Yes. I have given you the top five risks and what you have to avoid to be successful. I feel it is my obligation to also point out other mistakes that entrepreneurs usually make, so that I put you on the path of success. Mistakes are common, but if we know about them in advance, we would be able to avoid them. So, let's highlight the common mistakes you may make, but need to avoid from the very start, the ideation stage.

Image by John Hain from Pixabay

a. **Too many ideas**

Many entrepreneurs have this dilemma, they have too many business ideas. They like more than one idea that they want to start with. What to do in that situation? My advice is simple. You never know what will click and what would flop. You have to evaluate all of them and experiment a little bit. So, the trick is to let the idea marinate and you give yourself a grace period for research. Only move ahead with an idea if it comes up after your research. There are only a handful of entrepreneurs that can do more than one business idea really well. Well, all of us can't be Elon Musk. So, you have to give yourself a research period during which you have to pick only one. The point is that most of us can only do one thing really well. Think about it, if you give one thing a 100 percent focus, as soon as you have a second idea you can only give a part of your focus, like 50 percent to each. So, the results are always mediocre and you want to give the idea you choose 100 percent of your ability. Because even then it's still really hard. And keep in mind even with a 100 percent effort most businesses fail. But there's another way to look at this. What if most businesses fail precisely because they do not give them 100 percent of the effort? Some challenges are not easily surmountable while others are. And once you become aware of them some ideas will just naturally get disqualified. So really if you have too many business ideas this is the process you want to go through but you cannot be like I'm going to stay with multiple ideas.

b. **Too much theory**

There's only so much theoretical knowledge that you're going to get and theoretical feedback is just fine in theory. So, of course, you want to go around getting feedback from just about everybody. But every once in a while, it's actually better to test that idea by actually doing it. Because in case of many business ideas, it's feasible to start them quickly. It's okay to start small and cheaply so you can test the ideas.

But please keep in mind that you are starting them just to test as to how they are going to fare in the real world. Do not do this long-term. Be practical in your approach. Let me give you an example, if you really work hard and efficiently, it takes only a couple of days to put up a website or set up your profile somewhere where you want it to be. You could actually start your business, make some sales, get customers interested and activated. All this works if you are not starting something like a brick-and-mortar store or a restaurant. Of course, those take a long time but many other ideas, you can start them cheaply and quickly and you can definitely test them. So, it is really prudent to test your idea because it's going to give you a lot of lessons that theory just does not. But the core goal is to always pick one idea and focus on it do not lose sight of that.

> *"A lot of times people look at risk and ask, What are the odds that I will succeed? A different way to look at risk is to ask, What's the worst thing that would happen if I failed?"*
>
> *– Dave Hitz*

c. **Discipline**

So many people are not disciplined enough to take all the unnecessary things out of their lives to give the business more focus. Right? And it's not just your second or third business idea. Of course, you want to kill your second and third business ideas but what about irresponsible behavior. Getting high, drunk and wasted when you could be working? We basically tend to avoid work and use entertainment as an excuse. I might sound pedantic right now but hear me out. I have had my share of fun and frolic and don't look down upon having fun. What I am talking about is balance and discipline. You cannot succeed without discipline. Stop being influenced by superfluous movie culture where erratic behavior of a hero/heroine is branded as "cool". Be disciplined enough to maintain a balance between work and personal life. Having fun is essential, but overdoing it is going to be eventually cumbersome for you. Remember, you enjoy a real break and not when the break is your actual work. Every moment you waste is spent cutting time from your quota of time you had set aside for getting you towards your goals. That time gets freed up to work on your business. And actually, that's your goal. Free up as much time as possible for your work, without hurting your work-life balance. Making an effort with discipline is really important.

d. **Feedback**

The key to starting right is testing and getting the right feedback. Sometimes, you might just have a gut feeling that your idea is really going to work. There is nothing wrong with having a gut feeling. In fact, most of my ideas have started with me having a strong gut feel that it is going to work. You have to be able to trust the gut to a point. And even though you have to decide relatively quickly, don't decide impulsively. Feedback helps you curtail that impulse. Getting enough feedback is directly related to knowledge-based decisions. Talk to experts and when you talk to experts here's the question you should ask them. What are the biggest pitfalls in this business? Like what are the most challenging things? And when they tell you about those pitfalls, do keep those in your mind. You will be able to make calculated decisions on whether you could overcome those or whether they would be too hard for you. Feedback gives you signals and clues. And sometimes that's a clue, based on which your idea should either be pursued or thrown away.

> *"At the core of Silicon Valley is a passion for Yes!"*
>
> *– Steven Levy*

e. **Stress**

Stress is basically a feeling of emotional or physical tension. It can come from any event or thought that makes you feel frustrated, nervous or even angry. Stress is your body's reaction to a challenge or demand. In short quantities, stress could be positive, and at times it would help you avoid danger or meet certain deadlines. But mostly, stress has adverse effects. This is a very common experience shared by entrepreneurs. Stress is weighing on entrepreneurs, especially in the beginning. In fact, it is not just the stress, it's emotions like fear, anxiety low self-esteem, low confidence and so on. They all combine to make matters even worse. And that feeling stays there sometimes not for months but years until you get it right. We always hope the stressful situation does not last long, but usually; it takes us a long time to get out of that bad space where we struggle. It is the lack of things which normally plays on your minds, lack of money, lack of time, lack of support, lack of knowledge about what we're doing. Entrepreneurs are constantly making mistakes and trying to get out of those mistakes. This creates circumstances in which short-term decisions are made to relieve the short-term stress. So, these are more like a Band-Aid type of decisions. Short-sighted decisions are made just to get out of the stress because that's just the way our brain works. So, it all snowballs, but luckily, we have many stress relief techniques.

The only way to solve the issue of stress and not let it bother you is to have an abundance mentality. A person with an abundance mentality focuses on the limitless opportunities available in business and life. You need to focus on the positive things in your life rather than the negative things. People with an abundance mindset are more grateful, more creative and focused on collaboration. And these three elements together are the magic ingredients to get rid of stress.

So, here you have it. A complete point wise breakdown of the main risks you are going to face and the main limitations that are going to affect you. Overcome risk, make less mistakes and the world would seem like a better place. Not all would be solved but if you do adopt the right mindset, then definitely the journey seems easier and you would feel more confident in taking on the challenge. You have to face the realities, but instead of being bogged down by them, you have to embrace them. Three strong elements for success should never be forgotten – Gratitude, Creativity and Collaboration.

We continue our journey by understanding next the most important journey that affects all our businesses – the customer journey.

> *"I tell everybody, if you can cold-call once in your life, it's one of the best life trainings you can get. It's very humbling. It teaches you to be quick on your feet. It also teaches you not to take the word no so seriously. Face the rejection, and get back up and do it again. I would hear the word no all the time selling fax machines, so to me it just became like a numbers game."*
>
> *– Sara Blakely*

Chapter 7

CUSTOMER JOURNEY BLUEPRINT

> *"Amazing things will happen when you listen to the consumer."*
>
> – Jonathan Midenhall

True goes the saying "Customer is King!". Your understanding of your customer is the number 1 factor determining the success or failure of your venture. So, take the learning process and the understanding of your customer very seriously. So, who is your customer? Your customer is the person or a business that would be receiving, consuming or buying your products or services. They have all the scales tilted in their favor because they have the power of choice. They can easily choose someone else over you, simple yet powerful. Your main aim should be to attract your customers, and make them purchase what you have to offer.

Whether it's customer engagement, customer-service, customer-experience, customer management or, anything relating to customers. It is up to you to ensure they are better served. You should be constantly working on aspects to improve the user experience of your customer so that they purchase from you, give you repeat patronage and an excellent word of mouth. So, I will take you on a complete journey to understand your customer, their persona, their design, problems they face and culminate it with the most beneficial customer journey map. After going through this chapter, you would be better equipped for your business than ever before.

So, let's start.

Regardless of what industry you're in and what kinds of products and services you sell, the most important part of your business is going to be your customer. You won't see any sales, without the customer. As a result, they are a critical factor when developing your messaging and strategies. You should never fail to take into account customer's view, and if you do not, it is very likely that your business will not be successful.

So, the first thing to start with is to know your customer. When you have an idea of who they are and what they need, you can develop products or services that are tailored to helping your customers solve their problems more effectively. If you're not creating offerings based on customer needs, you may not be solving a real problem, offering a real solution and definitely won't be able to sell to them.

Knowing your customers also helps you to develop highly customized messaging that resonates with them. However, businesses often have many different kinds of customers, so it's difficult to know who you need to specifically target.

Tool 11: Segment your Customers and make Buyer Persona

One of the most effective ways you could use to understand your customers is to segment them based on specific criteria. It's very vital for you to understand that not all customers have the same needs or behave the same way toward your products or services. Keeping this in mind, you have to find an effective way to segment customers based on similar characteristics.

The four best ways to segment a customer based on similar characteristics are:

1. **Demographic:**

    This includes age, gender, sex, family status, occupation, income, race, nationality and other similar criteria. A married man with kids will need different approach than a senior male with no family.

2. **Geographic:**

    Where a customer lives would surely affect their needs and the challenges they face. Geographic criteria for segmentation include region, climate and population density. Someone living in a city will respond differently than someone living in a rural setting. A cold climate area like New York would have a different product or service need than a warm climate area like Florida, both part of the same country.

3. **Psychographic**:

    The main criterion here is about the lifestyle of the customer and includes aspects such as attitudes, opinions, interests and values. Someone who values their stand against child labor would not buy goods from places they know use child labor and would go for companies that have responsible manufacturing processes.

4. **Behavioural:**

    This segmentation criterion is all about how your customer would behave towards the product or service you would be offering. It includes the benefits they are looking for, how willing they are to buy, their loyalty and how often they use the product. How many times throughout the day do you think people make decisions? What should I wear today? What am I going to have for lunch? Think about it, people make many buying decisions every day without giving them much thought. You need to understand and segment them based on behavior.

Buyer Persona

Once you have segmented your customer, it is now time to create buyer personas. Buyer personas would help you understand your prospective customers in a much better way. This would make it easier for you to target your content, messaging, product and services to meet the specific needs and behaviors of the segmented audience. Create buyer personas of your key target market segments and also use these personas in mind when developing any marketing or sales campaigns. This will ensure you keep the customer at the top of your priority list.

A typical Buyer Persona would have 4 basic sections:

1. Background
2. Demographics
3. Behavior and Psychographics
4. Identifiers

Once you would have done your research with what I have written about audience segmentation, then the buyer persona would be really easy to make.

This is what a Buyer persona would read like:

- Person Name: Monica
- Is the Head of HR
- Has worked in this company for several years
- Was one of the first to join, is loyal
- Married with one kid, 12

- Female
- 38 years old
- Husband works. Have dual household income
- Lives in the suburbs
- Strong personality
- Has an assistant
- Likes things organized
- Wants email record or communication

Image by Gerd Altmann from Pixabay

Now that we have understood our customer, segmented them and the made the buyer persona, it is time to understand the typical problems customers have. Problems and pain points generate dissatisfaction. Try to eliminate this dissatisfaction through the solution that you offer and make the user experience as smooth as possible .

Typical Problems Customers Face

i. **Choice**

There are so many options available to customers that they are spoilt for choice. The world today is a real competitive place. Even when you feel you have no competition, you are just kidding yourself. Either there is existing competition or if you do get a little success, be rest assured people will try to copy your success formula. So always try to stay ahead of the game and try to address the choice of your customer. So that they come to you as opposed to your competitor.

ii. **Explore**

Once the consumer makes a choice, like say they were thinking of what to eat and decide to eat Mexican food. Now comes the exploration part where they look for options to find the right place to eat. Your part is to be visible, known and be there when they come exploring.

iii. **Ease of Use**

Ease of use is linked to your ability to be able to offer maximum functionality. In a way it is to optimize the user experience while respecting the limitations of your business. Your customer has made their choice and found you after exploring other options, now it is your turn to make their interaction points with you as convenient as possible.

iv. **Belief and Trust**

We live in a high maintenance, skeptical world. Customers tend to have trust issues and may doubt your ability to deliver. The mantra is to have the ability to live up to expectations. If you have promised something in your offer, the closer you get to fulfilling your commitments, the closer you are to winning over someone. You get a customer's trust and if they start to believe in you, be rest assured you would be getting repeat business and a lot of good word of mouth.

v. **Barrier to entry**

   Apart from the four main problem areas a consumer would face, there are other general barriers to entry of a business which keeps the customer away. Price, time and convenience are three most common barriers to entry. You make sure that your product or service is offered at the right price, your processes are convenient and it takes the shortest possible time for the delivery. To get it right, always know the limitations of your business and offer only what you can satisfactorily deliver.

So, there you have it. We understand our customer and have segmented them, got personas and understand their pain points and the problems they face. Now let us go to a very important aspect, in which we will detail every point of interaction your customer has with your business at different stages.

Tool 12: Customer Journey Map

A customer journey map is a visual representation of the customer journey that they take when they interact with your business. You consider all the touch points and try to tell the story of your customer's experiences with your product or service. Mapping out the customer journey visually helps ensure a greater understanding of your customer and in turn the subsequent success of your company. You could use this map for your future campaigns too.

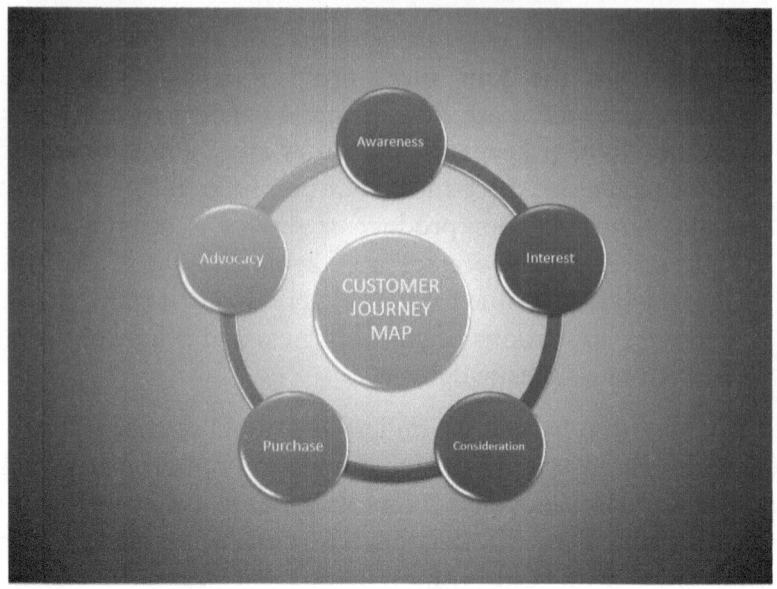

Illustration by Gaurav Vasishta

If you can take a quick peek at the graphical representation of the customer journey map. To do this right, you should consider the problems that generate dissatisfaction for your customer. Start from Awareness and end at Advocacy. You will see that there are five main stages of a customer's journey.

STAGE 1: AWARENESS

This is the stage where your customer becomes aware of your product. They realize they have a problem/need/desire. Awareness happens through self-induced discovery, search, an advertisement, word of mouth etc. You have to outline how and where your customer becomes aware of your product or service and whether at that point of interaction you have ensured there is enough attraction in your offer to make them interested.

Stage 2: Interest

This is where now your customer wants the product or service you offer. You have made them aware but now they would be searching (remember choice?), they start reading reviews, make comparisons, ask for opinions, and explore their options. So here you have to see how and where do customers search for detailed information about your product or service. You have to make sure that you can stimulate their interest buds enough to consider you as at least one of their top five choices. Comparison charts with competition, reviews etc. really help at this stage.

Stage 3: Consideration

You have generated interest. Now you would have to nail the consideration part where your customer is making their decision between most likely purchases, taking product demonstrations, asking for opinions from previous users, etc. So, you would be considering how and where do customers decide to purchase your product or service. Your consideration effort should be solid and enticing enough, as it leads to a sale!

Stage 4: Purchase

Ring in the cash registers! This is where your customer actually buys your product or service. You have been good enough to generate interest and they have considered buying your product. This is where efficiency kicks in. Make the buying process smooth. You definitely can't get your interaction points wrong when it is purchase time. So look at payment gateways, steps it takes, value ads, etc. to ensure your customer leaves smiling and satisfied after buying.

Stage 5: Advocacy

Don't rest and settle just because you have managed to make a sale. Once the client has bought a product/service, they will surely form an opinion. You have to ensure two things here. The first one I have mentioned before – commit only what you can deliver! The second one is to ensure that you have enough communication and interaction with your customers. Feedback is a must, not only so that you could fill any voids in fulfillment, but also for improvement. Word of mouth or referrals have the highest conversion rates. Get it right.

So there you have it. The wonderful customer journey map that you need to make to get a visual representation of your interactions with your customer. Note each stage down and use it to improve user satisfaction.

We have to finish by emphasizing the importance of a customer to an organization. There isn't a business in the world that would survive without customers. Customers are not only responsible for giving you the revenue but they also give you the requisite brand recognition and awareness. They are the foundation of your business. It's extremely important to not just seek and attract new customers but also to retain existing ones, too. Customers are always exploring new options even if they have their favorites. And that's a great opportunity for you to inform them that they have other options.

The cornerstone of our business should be to identify, satisfy, and retain our customers. This is what lays the groundwork for what has become a strategic imperative in modern marketing; customer relationship management.

To a student of marketing in the digital age, the idea of a relationship formed between customers and businesses may seem obvious and commonplace. It definitely is an extension of the marketing concept, which guides businesses towards understanding and addressing customer needs. But only in recent times has technology made it possible for us to capture and utilize information about our customers to this scale and extent. Data science and analytics are household terms today. The Internet and digital social media have created new platforms for communication between the businesses and their customers. As a result, there are more tools now than ever before which help companies create, maintain, and manage customer relationships. Use these tools for the analysis of your customer. You can work on existing data and the data that you generate and create through your own interactions with your customer. Have an effective customer relationship management and be rest assured it would reduce the cost of business and increase your profitability.

In the end, just remember that winning new customers would take a significant amount of time, effort, and resources. Be strong and keep working on building a solid foundation. Knowledge, strategy and focused effort always leads to success.

> *"Advertising brings in customers, but word-of-mouth brings in the best customers."*
>
> *– Jonah Berger*

Chapter 8

BOOST PRODUCTIVITY

> *"Focus on being productive instead of busy."*
> *– Tim Ferriss*

I'm a little bit of a geek and aware about two topics – emotional intelligence and productivity. I love this stuff for entrepreneurship because those are the soft skills that make a real big difference in your business. So, for me, writing about this is going to be fun. I will give you an introduction to emotional intelligence, and then discuss some productivity principles and then we shall do an exercise for you to immediately begin implementing this stuff. Making small changes to habits will drastically improve the levels of productivity and efficiency in your business. This will allow you to get more quality work done as well as reduce the amount of time spent.

BOOST PRODUCTIVITY

Image by Gerd Altmann from Pixabay

Emotional Intelligence

What happens when you get your business idea? You get excited of course! Yeah. So, excitement is a really common emotion. And with this let's start discussing emotional intelligence. What do we know about excitement? Well, it's a double-edged sword. It's a positive emotion for most people, it gives you a feeling of great enthusiasm and eagerness. It gives you immediate motivation. But therein lies the negative side of excitement, short-term motivation. What we get is not the real path for your business to be successful. For that, we require long-term motivation. So, excitement is great to get us going but it is not what we exactly need. And the other issue with excitement is that we tend to overestimate things which can be misleading. We tend to overestimate the potential for our business success and underestimate our potential struggles. So, in a way we are actually deceiving ourselves into starting something we maybe shouldn't be starting.

So, the point here is that we need to understand emotional intelligence or emotional quotient and then use our learning to plan a little better and build certain beneficial habits. So, what is emotional intelligence? It is basically your ability to understand, manage and effectively use your own emotions in a positive way to communicate effectively, ease your stress, identity and overcome challenges and handle relationships better.

According to Daniel Goleman, the American psychologist who helped popularize emotional intelligence, there are five key elements to it:

- Self-awareness.
- Self-regulation.
- Motivation.
- Empathy.
- Social skills.

So I have used the same principles and put together ways to develop your emotional intelligence.

1. **Self Awareness**

    Self-awareness is the ability to see yourself clearly and objectively through introspection and reflection. When you're able to manage and reduce your negative emotions, you're less likely to get overwhelmed. Self-awareness is an important factor at play in how we think, how we feel, and how we act and how we react. Self-awareness allows us to see things from the perspective of others, practice self-control, add creativity and productivity to our work, and experience better self-esteem. Practice mindfulness at work, and notice how your perspective changes.

2. **Self Regulation**

    Self-regulation, in the most basic sense, is about controlling one's behavior, emotions, and thoughts in the pursuit of long-term goals. More specifically, emotional self-regulation refers to your ability to manage troublesome emotions and impulses. Everyone encounters challenges. It's your reaction to these challenges that either sets you up for success or puts you on the track for failure. You already know that positive thinking will counter adversity. The trick to counter adversity is to practice optimism instead of complaining.

3. **Motivation**

   Self-motivation is the force that drives you to do things. The ability to keep encouraging yourself to continue making progress towards a goal, even when it feels challenging. I like to call it the movement from "I should do it" to "I must do it!" You need to ignite that inner fire and drive to develop, produce, achieve and keep progressing. When you just don't know how to start or after starting your business you have come to a stage where you're thinking of quitting, your self-motivation is what pushes you to go on and keep you on track.

4. **Empathy**

   Empathy helps us understand how others would be feeling so we can respond appropriately to them in every situation. Be it verbal or non-verbal cues, they can give you invaluable insight into the feelings of others. Practice the art of focusing on others and try to put yourself in their shoes, even if just for a moment. Empathetic statements do not excuse unacceptable behavior, just keep in mind that everyone has their own issues. Always acknowledge in some way how the other person might feel.

5. **Social skills**

   Focus on becoming a stronger communicator wherever you might be working. You have to work on four aspects;

social skills, communication, gestures, body language and your appearance. This changes significantly online as we have to adjust to the nuances of online social skills. Emotionally intelligent people tend to use more specific words that can help communicate better. Being appropriate is very important along with the age-old mantra – healthy interactions lead to great relationships. Take stock of what stresses you out, and be proactive to have less of it in your life. The way to do it is what I mentioned in the last chapter – have an abundance mentality.

Emotional intelligence is something that evolves, as long as you have the desire. It takes practice, but you can start reaping the benefits immediately. Having a high level of emotional intelligence will serve you well in your relationships in the workplace and in all areas of your life. Would you like that?

> *"What really matters for success, character, happiness and lifelong achievements is a definite set of emotional skills – your EQ – not just purely cognitive abilities that are measured by conventional IQ tests."*
>
> *– Daniel Goleman*

Tool 13: Boosting Productivity

I realized very long ago that there was nothing exciting about the daily routine that I had working on my business. It got to the level of being borderline boring. I learned a lesson and am going to share with you the same in three simple words – Live with it! Like my business, your business might be boring too. I normally am just sitting with my computer typing away. Nothing glamorous about it. Can't really complain and cry about your work and what puts bread on the table, even though it's not the most exciting thing in the world. I don't have excitement every moment of my day. Regular things are just regular. So, what I did was, I formulated a way that boring did not disturb or bother me. I formed a routine. I made working into a habit, and that is exactly what you need. What you need is for your work to become a habit for you.

Keep postponing things and you have the disease I call procrastination. This starts the moment excitement goes away. Procrastination takes place due to many reasons but primarily because the actual work is boring. Some people are just plain lazy, but laziness does not get you success. So, how are we going to overcome procrastination and laziness that creeps in? We're going to build you a healthy habit. One of the very first things, when I start talking about productivity, is reversing or stopping procrastination. We are going to formulate a way to introduce a healthier behavior and habits and work on incremental improvements using the *Kanban method*.

Normally, habits are usually built when you do something every day for two or three weeks. It's easier to build bad habits and it's much harder to build good habits. You already knew that. So, for three weeks we're going to build you a healthy habit. And what I'd like you to do as your exercise is actually really important and will help you in boosting productivity.

So, this is what I would like you to do. Follow these 6 basic principles and make them into a healthy habit:

1. **One Task at a time:** We are not meant to be doing multiple tasks at a time. Multitasking reduces productivity considerably. When we toggle between tasks our focus becomes limited, our reflexes and working productivity is affected and in turn it also causes stress and mental fatigue. So boost your productivity by focusing on only one task at a time. We have to accept the fact that it is not humanly possible to multitask. You get more done if you are able to allocate time to each

task and complete it during that time. Efficient and productive. Don't over-commit and set your priorities to know what needs to be done and in what order. It is always tempting to accomplish more at once but that is just less productive.

Habit 1: Focus on a single task at a time, and you'll actually end up completing it faster.

2. **Eliminate Digital Distractions:** Do you frequently check your phone during work or social settings? With the smart phone entering our lives, an average person has started spending nearly one-quarter of their workday browsing social media and other digital distractions for non-work-related activities. I am not trying to say that occasional browsing through social media is a bad thing, but you need to allocate time for digital surfing, be it social media or you browsing shoes on amazon. After allocating time, you need to then stick to it and make it a habit not to browse and give in to that urge to see updates. Constantly checking your phone for updates hampers productivity in a big way. Set a limit on the amount of time you spend on the net. Also, disable app notifications and mute updates. Anything that limits the interruptions or temptations caused by technology will help you stay focused and boost your productivity.

Habit 2: Control and remove Digital distractions and make a surfing schedule.

3. **Seize the first two hours**: You would find it a little strange but the first two hours of the day are the most critical for productivity and this has been scientifically proven. This time, the first two hours, is the ideal time to set and review your goals for the day, tackle the most challenging and critical thing that needs to be done, and take a personal moment to do what matters to

you most. By seizing and maximizing those first few hours, you can transform your entire day. So, think of the most crucial task on your to do list and instead of procrastinating, do it first.

Habit 3: Develop the lifelong habit of tackling your major task in the first few hours of your day.

4. **Break big tasks into smaller ones**: It used to stress me out just looking at the pending projects on my calendar, those days hanging on a wall. When I started setting smaller goals, they seemed doable and also by finishing something I started getting a sense of achievement. Looking at big goals or projects at hand could be overwhelming. So break them into small components, smaller tasks. By doing so you would feel more in control and will end up being much more productive. This will keep you on track and make the bigger projects seem less daunting.

Habit 4: Set small goals for yourself by breaking bigger projects into smaller mini tasks.

5. **Take regular breaks**: Your mind needs to be refreshed and refueled from time to time. This maximizes your efficiency and boosts concentration, creativity and memory. Working without a break leads to stress, exhaustion and affects your decision-making capabilities. You might think that by working longer hours you would be getting more done, but on the contrary, we work much better if we take regular breaks to refresh ourselves. Regular breaks from work help your concentration and boost your productivity.

Habit 5: Take short and regular breaks from work.

6. **Get enough sleep**: Sleep is a very vital, often neglected, part of every person's overall health and productivity. Sleep is important because it enables

your body to repair and be fit and ready for another day at work. They say getting seven to nine hours of sleep in 24 hours is crucial for your physical and mental well-being. You would be more prone to errors and your efficiency would be greatly reduced if you are sleep deprived. So, it might sound simple, but if you want to boost productivity, boost creativity and reduce stress, just sleep properly.

Habit 6: Be regular in your sleep patterns and ensure you get enough sleep.

So that's your exercise. Do these 6 changes in your lifestyle and work style and you would find your self more efficient and your productivity significantly improved. You need to make working on your business a habit because the path to success is long term productive work. And that's exactly going to be achieved through building these 6 habits.

> *"Action is the foundational key to all success."*
>
> *– Picasso*

Tool 14: The Kanban Method

The Kanban Method is an efficient process to gradually improve whatever you do – whether it is software development, IT, Operations, Staffing, Recruitment, Marketing and Sales, Procurement, etc. I wanted to put it out there because I have been using it for many years and find it an absolute game-changer when it comes to a productivity boost. It would be worthwhile to note that almost any business process can benefit from applying the principles of the Kanban Methodology.

KANBAN PRINCIPLES & PRACTICES

The Kanban Method follows a set of principles and practices for workflow. It helps you to manage and improve the flow of work. I find it evolutionary and a non-disruptive method that induces gradual improvements to an organization's processes. If you follow the Kanban principles and practices, you will be able to successfully benefit your business process – be it improving the flow of work, reducing cycle times, increasing value to the customer and you would be able to do all this with greater predictability. This would be very beneficial for your business, always.

The Concept of Kanban

Kanban is an evolutionary non-disruptive management system of change. This means that the existing process is improved incrementally. Rather than making huge changes, the idea is to implement many minor changes. What this does is it reduces risk to the overall system. This non-disruptive approach ensures that the team and other stakeholders involved offer low or no resistance to the changes.

So, let's get to it step-by-step as it is important for you to understand the concept to be able to implement it. The first step of Kanban is to visualize the workflow. This is done in the form of a Kanban board consisting of a simple whiteboard and sticky notes or cards. You could do this in other ways as well, including digitally. Just remember that each card on the board represents a task.

In a classic Kanban board model, there are three columns:

To Do: This column lists the tasks that are not yet started.

Doing: This consists of the tasks that are in progress.

Done: This consists of the tasks that are completed.

This simple visualization of the workflow is a transparent way to understand the distribution of the work as well as existing bottlenecks. The possibilities of the Kanban boards are limitless as you work on elaborate workflows depending on their complexity. You can always examine specific parts of the workflow to identify bottlenecks in order to remove them.

THE CONCEPT OF FLOW

At the core of Kanban is the concept of Flow. Just like a river meanders along its path, just visualize a flow of the processes and make sure that this flow is maintained. This means that the cards or tasks should flow through the system as evenly as possible, without long waiting times or blockages. Everything that hinders the flow should be immediately examined and dealt with. Kanban has different techniques, metrics and models, and if these are consistently applied, it can lead to a culture of continuous improvement (kaizen). Kaizen is a Japanese term meaning "change for the better" or continuous improvement.

The concept of Flow is crucial and by measuring the Flow metrics and making improvements, you can increase the speed of your delivery processes while decreasing cycle times and enhancing the quality of your products or services. To stop hindrances, you are also pushed into getting relevant and faster feedback from your customers, be it internal or external.

Once we have understood the concept of flow, now we get to the four foundational principles of Kanban and then I will give you the six Core Practices of the Kanban Methodology:

FOUR FOUNDATIONAL PRINCIPLES OF KANBAN

Start with what you are doing now: Non-disruptive. Your approach to Kanban needs to follow the principle of non-disruption to the existing setup/process. So you should not be making any change to your existing setup/process right away. Kanban must be applied directly to the current workflow. So, any changes needed have to be introduced gradually over a period of time and in small steps.

Agree to pursue incremental, change: Continuing on the first principle of starting with what you have, the next crucial step is to understand that you have to be mentally prepared and in turn prepare your team and associated members to agree to and accept small changes. This would ensure you would have very little resistance within the organization when you implement Kanban. Just remember to make small incremental changes rather than making radical changes.

Start with respecting current roles and responsibilities: Kanban does not impose any organizational changes by itself. So before you start finding faults and think of changing the entire team, look at the structure, roles and responsibilities. There might be existing roles and functions which may be performing well. Encourage the team to collaboratively identify and implement any changes needed.

Encourage acts of leadership at all levels: There is no point in having a great founder if he does not have a great team that works collaboratively and efficiently. This needs leadership at all levels and not only at the top. Kanban encourages continuous improvement at all levels of the organization. Leadership acts don't have to originate from senior managers only. Ideas can come from anywhere. Introspection of an organization happens when people at all levels are allowed to provide ideas and show leadership. Once this happens, it is easier to implement changes to continually improve the way you would deliver your products and services.

These four principles help organizations overcome the typical emotional resistance and the fear of change that usually accompany any reform initiatives in an organization.

Now, coming to the actual Kanban board, there are 5 different columns that you can start building. Stories, To Do, In Progress, Testing, Done. Build a board (many online versions are available these days). Choose online Kanban boards with cards to communicate statuses, progress, and issues. If offline, you could have a board with stickies or cards with different colors to signify either different classes of service or could be simply the different type of work items. Then we make the above five columns and start filling in the cards.

Stories: These are basically backlogs. So you start your board by gathering and then prioritizing your product backlog. Add a Product Owner and make it their task, the responsibility of gathering and prioritization of user stories. This person can be defined as a representative of the customer. Kanban projects require strong customer involvement to perform them quickly, so the Product Owner must participate in the team's work constantly. User Stories, with the right size that are testable, result in development and testing within specified time limits.

To do: If you think about it, Kanban boards are big to-do lists that display all the work that awaits you. Since tasks are distributed in columns according to the process stage they are in, your 'To do' column is your actual to-do list. Plus, cards are usually color coded and ordered by priority. So you would automatically know what is the next task you should focus on.

In Progress: When you move from the To Do list to the right, you put your card in the 'In Progress' column. It would be worthwhile here to understand the concept of Kanban WIP and the WIP Limits. WIP is Work-in-Progress. The WIP Limits are defined at each stage of the workflow on a Kanban board to encourage team members and all involved to finish work at hand and only then, take up the next set of work. This is because the key feature of Kanban is to reduce the amount of multi-tasking that most teams and associated partners are prone to do. There is an interesting encouragement I had read which said "Stop Starting! And Start Finishing!", a mantra coined by Dr. Arne Roock (of www.Software-Kanban.de). This encouragement needs to be given to all associated with your workflow. Typically, you should start with a WIP Limit of 1 or 1.5 times the number of people working in a specific stage. Putting the WIP limits on each column of the board helps the team first finish what they are doing before taking up new stuff.

Testing: We have learnt earlier in stories that all the possible behaviors of the system are captured by means of User Stories, which should be testable and effectively sized. Size of the User Stories allow Development and Testing to be complete within the Iteration. So we have to focus on continuous Integration testing and also prevent defects with the test cases. So, if we use WIP limits to focus on a limited number of User Stories/ To Do at a time, our testing too becomes smoother and better.

Done: Sounds good right? Done. This is your backlog "Stories" flow from "To Do" to "Work in Progress" to "Testing" what is produced to being Done! What you need to remember is to specify the definition of "Done" criteria for each Kanban column. So you need to make processes and policies explicit and ensure that before another task is added to the work in progress, your team would have completed essential tasks.

So there you have a Kanban Board. Just remember a few pointers like managing flow by highlighting the various stages of the workflow and the status of work in each stage. You will be able to identify bottlenecks if you see a break in flow or work piling up at one column, but only if your WIP Limits are set. So remember to manage the flow of work from to the end of the workflow. Kanban helps your team analyze the system and its behavior to allow you to make adjustments to improve flow. This would lead to a huge productivity boost as you would now be using less time to complete each piece of work.

KANBAN BOARD

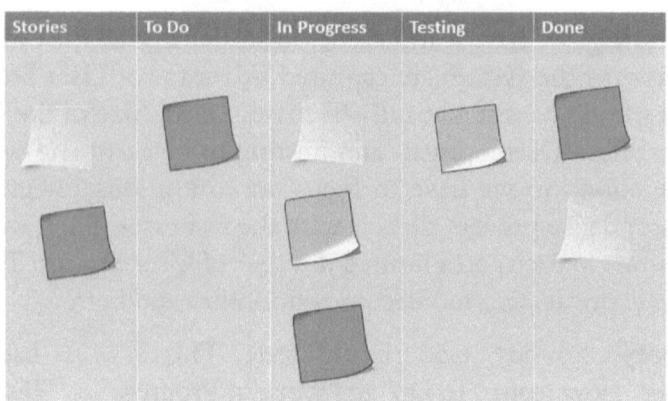

Image by Gaurav Vasishta

Kanban, also spelt "kamban" in Japanese, translates to "Billboard" that indicates "available capacity (to work)".

So, this chapter has been all about harnessing your strengths, your emotional intelligence and learning to make incremental changes in your value stream, your habits, methodology and then learning smart ways to boost your productivity. Keep implementing what you have read in this chapter and you would be able to effectively improve many aspects of your business, be it the delivery of your products and services, eliminating bottlenecks in your system, improving flow and reducing cycle time and most importantly, boosting your productivity. Because, as they say, an increase in productivity is always an opportunity for growth.

> "If you spend too much time thinking about a thing, you'll never get it done."
>
> – Bruce Lee, actor

Chapter 9

SALES & MARKETING

It all boils down to Marketing & Sales. You add to it Digital Marketing and you have what it takes to be successful in today's world. This is the age of the customer. Today's marketing and sales needs to be aligned together. Marketing and Sales always need to complement each other. That is why I have combined the two together in this chapter and added Digital marketing to make it completely relevant for today's businesses. So let me start with laying the groundwork with the Marketing Plan.

MARKETING PLAN:

If ever you wanted to utilize a business tool, it has got to be the Marketing Plan. Not only does it become your go to document, it will also help you in your introduction and presentation to the outside world. So, let's say you are looking for funding for your start-up, any lender or investor, would want to see your marketing plan to understand the stability of the revenue model and how their money is going to generate a positive return. If you are looking to take your business to the next level, or if you have already reached a level and want to sell equity, your potential acquirers will definitely want to understand both your marketing plan and your marketing strategy.

So what is this marketing plan? Well, the planning is used to define the role and responsibilities of the marketing team, keeping in mind the achievement of goals of the business. After allocation of roles and responsibilities comes the allocation of resources for marketing, so that they can be utilized most beneficially and economically. After that comes operations. A plan needs to give direction for the operations. Finally, the planning would involve the preparation of policies, programs, budgets and other aspects and functions of marketing.

Planning and strategy are necessary to build your empire. The marketing and growth of a company depend on traction. What is important in achieving this traction is growing your customer base, retaining those customers and ensuring you serviced them well enough for them to refer your product or service to others. To be counted as a successful company, you need to have a plan that gives you this traction and growth.

Get the Product right. To get the best out of your marketing plan and strategy, remember not to lose sight of the basic foundation first. Traction and growth come when the product and service is actually good. So first things first. Work on a killer product or service. Your growth is not only related to your marketing, outreach, or sales efforts but to the product itself. If you are just starting up, then your product or service will probably be far from perfect. So, first work on that with your marketing and sales team, who have the feedback from customers, to perfect that product.

One of your very first hires should be the marketing person if you are not doing it on your own. There should be marketing feedback and a marketing perspective in all your business functions from the very beginning. Have all the marketing planning from early stages and involve the marketing team with all decisions in development, conversion, designing, picking out which features to develop, etc. Marketing is never to be considered an expense, it's always an investment.

This book is about tools. So I am not going to explain further how to write a marketing plan. What I am going to jump into is what matters and what you are looking for. What works? How do I make a campaign? What channels do I use? Yes, we are going to go through the theory as before to understand the concepts, but as always, I will keep hopping over to the practical aspects of your business.

Image by Gerd Altmann from Pixabay

Tool 15: Marketing Strategy and Channels:

The entire marketing strategy should be based on your customer. I did an entire chapter on the Customer just for this. Knowing your customer is the backbone of your marketing and sales strategy. So, answer these three questions with what you have learnt in the chapter on Customer Blueprint.

1. Who is your target customer for the solution and value proposition you are going to offer?

2. What are the characteristics, attributes and buyer's persona of this customer?

3. Where do I find this customer?

Your product and service is meant for a particular customer segment and your entire marketing strategy is going to be based on reaching this customer. Your price model is based on the same customer. This is the customer for whom you are solving the pain points efficiently. This is the customer who buys your product to give you revenue and traction as early as possible. This is the customer that fits your value proposition, your business model, and other characteristics. Know your customer and you already have 50% of your marketing strategy.

There is a saying "Fish where the fishes are". This basically means after understanding who your customer is and their persona, you need to now understand where you would find this customer. What channels are you going to use to reach out to this customer? Finding customers is one of the most difficult challenges for any businesses. Just because you have started a business does not mean that the customers will find you, your store, your website your channel. You are the one who has to go out and find potential customers. You need customer acquisition as the focus for your business. That is your marketing strategy.

Innovation: You have to remember that marketing strategies need to be backed up by innovation in your approach. There are a few things you could do to be innovative, like making bold statements, living your brand, being cool about competition, making yourself newsworthy and being a socially responsible brand. If you are able to compliment your marketing strategy with innovation you will see tremendous growth in your business. This is a modern take on marketing.

Positioning Statement: The concept of modern marketing is based on standing out from the crowd. If you have a new product and a new venture, it is very important for you to be perceived differently and get noticed. So, from the beginning have a clear positioning statement. The goal is to take all that is great about your product, your value proposition, your offer and couple it with information about your competitors and industry and consolidate it into one useful document. It will be helpful to you in every aspect of your marketing strategy. If you try to market everything to everybody, you end up with nothing. So, it is very important to have a positioning statement to help you understand what makes you different and unique in comparison with your competition and why should customers buy your product or service. It helps you understand where and for whom you are faster, better, cheaper, more effective or more efficient.

Channels to Use: If you want to market a product or service to your customer, you need method or a platform – this is what a channel is. The whole idea behind using a channel is to acquire the customer and ensure consumption. I have done the hard work for you and am giving you the list of 10 Channels that are the best for any company to acquire customers. From within these 10 marketing channels, you can choose and create campaigns around them. These channels are:

1. **Public Relations**: Good PR is really an art. Get your brand name visible in blogs, newspapers, press publications, publicity stunts etc.

2. **Social Media Display Ads**: Facebook/Instagram/Twitter/LinkedIn/Reddit/Pinterest ads should be based on your customer's interests. Use the platform using the audience design we covered in Customer Journey Blueprint.

3. **Search Engine Marketing**: SEM, PPC are all great ways to drive relevant traffic. You should use search engines like Google, Bing or even YouTube.

4. **Offline Ads**: Yes we live in an online world, but never underestimate the power of offline ads. I started with these and still use them extensively. Radio commercials,

billboards, infomercials, TV spots, newspaper and magazine ads etc.

5. **Search Engine Optimization**: This is a little complex. Mostly relevant for Google and how they rank your website. Well, if they change the algorithm, you adapt accordingly.

6. **Content Marketing**: You need to be able to create, publish, and distribute content for a targeted audience online. This really works if done well as is a focused channel.

7. **Email Marketing**: I find this channel very effective especially with the tools available these days to create funnels and automated responses.

8. **Blogs & Vlogs**: Either create a Blog or Vlog or use existing blogs or vlogs as influencer marketing. The idea is to reach out to niche audiences.

9. **Affiliate Programs**: These surprisingly work. You are basically offering rewards to your customers to refer your product or service.

10. **Events**: Hosting an online event these days is not difficult. Use platforms like Meetup, Facebook etc. Even host offline events, participate in trade shows, have speaking engagements etc.

And, that's it. Ten marketing channels for the growth of your company. Use this curated list. We now move onto the sales part. Sales equates to the revenue generated and this revenue covers your expenses. Sales allows you to create stable operations and have a clear opportunity for growth while covering your expenses.

> *"Your top of the funnel content must be intellectually divorced from your product but emotionally wed to it."*
>
> – Joe Chernov

Image by Peggy from Pixabay

Tool 16: Sales & Lead Generation:

While marketing was all about acquiring and retaining the customers, sales is more transaction-based. The functions and process are different for marketing and sales, although they share a common goal of increasing the company's revenue. Marketing would cover all activities starting with the market research and ending with consumer satisfaction. Basically, sales is a part of marketing and an exchange or a transaction has taken place between you and the customer, mostly monetary. Sales is all about fulfilling the needs of the business – the sales targets.

So, let's learn the art of pushing the company's products and services onto the customers, by convincing them to buy.

Now let's get to the phase of sales. The first step is the scariest and the most beautiful memory – the first sale. I still remember the name of my first customer from 1998! (Andrew). The scary part is the uncertainty because you have spent all this time building the product, you don't know if people would accept it and pay for it. If your fundamentals are strong and you have followed the process of building your startup, you would have ensured that the development of your product or service was done by identifying a problem in society and you have come up with a solution with your product, keeping in mind the target market. So, you should not worry whether people would like to buy it or not. People will buy, but you need to know how to sell to them.

Sales plan and strategy needs to be built, and building sales from scratch should start with the sales team. Remember we had talked about multitasking and the adverse affects it has on productivity? Similarly, it is important to have a focused team for different responsibilities. If you start and are also the sales person for your team, then ensure that you dedicate ample amount of time for sales and when you are selling, you are only selling! If you are hiring for sales, then you should be very selective and should select only those personnel who have the ability and are willing to drive revenue for your business. When I started, my experience was that a sales team initially is not necessary but is only required at a later stage if the demand grows for your product or service, which would mean having more leads than your current setup could handle. Another way to look at it is revenue i.e., if you are earning enough revenue and could afford to hire a full-time sales personnel then the decision should be to go for a sales team, albeit small. Before expanding your members, test the waters to see how your target customer audience is responding to your product/service.

Sales Engine: When you start building out your sales team, your first worry might be that you are doing it wrong, second would be that you might be digging your own hole and third would be the performance of the person you will hire. That is why it is important to build a sales engine. In order to increase revenues of a business, it is necessary to have a good sales team and retain them. Remember that every time you recruit, you incur training and development cost. So, building a sales engine is a better approach. Performance & Retention of good sales personnel being the key.

So, how do you build a sales engine? Start with these four basics:

1. **Salary**: There is a tendency of everyone who hires to link the payout to commissions and performance. But remember we want to have performance and retention in our sales engine, so do cover some level of basic salary. A basic salary instills confidence in your team and makes them feel as if you are investing in them. The main focus of a sales person should not be worrying about the paycheck, but on the revenue growth of the company. Training and learning the ropes to hardwire oneself to sell.

2. **Targets**: It is really important to have a target for sales. When you are dividing the targets, also have a quota for each sales member. It is important to not put pressure, as when people are starting off, there is a good chance they are not going to hit the target that you have set. You should look performance as a percentage of quota that is achieved, and over time you will notice that the percentage goes up and up. So, understand the targets and quotas as per your industry standards and set them for your team.

3. **Commissions**: It is very important to be rewarded for performance. The variable compensation drives a sales person to achieve more as it affects his lifestyle directly. The more he or she makes, the more they are able to improve their lifestyle in return. So, you pay them a percentage of their pay based on sales that they're making. There is no better motivation than money itself. Keep pushing to ensure that your sales team aligns their performance with incentives and that would drive your business forward. Keep increasing the commission component on exceeding targets and quotas.

4. **Referral, Network & Miss-selling**: I have combined these three inter-related aspects of sales. You should know that the highest conversion rates are when someone refers your product or service to their known. The power of referrals can never be underestimated and the sales team should always be encouraged to ask for referrals and in turn increase the network for your company. But what we need to understand is that a sales person leaves a customer with a certain level of expectation from the product or service and it is imperative that these expectations are met for the customer to ever consider referring you. So, if you ever want a referral and your network to grow, you have to ensure that the sales team does not misrepresent the product or service in any way through expectations. No miss-selling, no false expectations.

Forecasting: If you want to achieve ultimate sales, you need to learn the art of forecasting. So you need to be able to estimate future revenue by providing a guidance on the sales revenues for your product or service. This needs to be done for your entire sales team and should be divided by month, quarter and year. What this does is that it would allow you to efficiently allocate resources and manage your cash flow for future growth.

> *"Refuse to attach a negative meaning to the word 'no.' View it as feedback. 'No' tells you to change your approach, create more value or try again later."*
>
> – Anthony Iannarino

LEAD GENERATION:

One main area where new entrepreneurs initially face a lot of difficulty is generating leads. You start off with first few leads which are mostly people you know. You need to have a pipeline of inquiries from potential customers. It is very important to have lead generation and use as many channels as possible to ensure that your pipelines remain full. Both quality and quantity are important factors, as this is the first step of your sales process. Quality leads would be the ones that a salesperson has a good chance of closing. Any lead which has a potential to become a customer should be important for us. Of course, there would be a number of bad leads of people who are not even qualified to buy the product or service, but it would come down to the numbers game. You would need a pipeline of leads and your sales would be a percentage of those leads. The higher the percentage, higher the quality. So, the technique you use to generate leads should be a trade-off between quality and quantity. It is important to use a different lead generation methods.

Whatever your product or service, whatever your segment, whether B2C or B2B, you need to have lead generation methodology and divide the process into components. There are four basic components for lead generation:

a. **Lead Capture:** This strategy is used to collect information from a lead. For B2C it is information like their name, contact information and relevant demographics qualifying details. For B2B it is information like business name, position, number of employees and other relevant firmographics.

b. **Lead Magnets**: This strategy is to attract a prospect by providing incentives. Baiting should be extensively used to generate interest.

c. **Lead Qualification**: You need to be able to qualify a lead as quality or junk. So this component takes all the information available at hand and tries to determine the likelihood of a sale from the lead.

d. **Lead Segmentation**: Once you have the leads by capture and attraction through lead magnets, and you have qualified the leads, then you should segment the leads based on their information, habits, and activities.

Every lead ends up in a funnel. The more you pour in, the more likelihood of increasing sales, as in a funnel the actual closed sale is a small percentage of the leads provided.

Once we have understood the different components, we need to also learn the methods that can be used to actually generate leads.

Some of the lead generation methods you could use are:

1. SEO and SEM - Search Engine Optimization & Marketing
2. PPC - Pay Per Click
3. Website
4. Landing Page
5. SMO and SMM - Social Media Optimization & Marketing
6. Webinars

7. Blogs
8. Marketing Videos and Reels
9. Advertising
10. Email Marketing
11. E-books, Newsletters, White Papers, etc.
12. Events & Meetups
13. Referral Rewards program

There are plenty more methods for lead generation. Choose as many as you can effectively execute to get as many leads as you possibly can, preferably quality leads. Keep a consistent way to track and rank your leads once you get them. You have to keep track of key information about each prospective buyer and evaluate them based on how likely they are to buy. You also need to be recording a lead's buying behavior which will guide you in taking many business decisions. So you must follow up with your prospective buyers and try to keep a track of what they have communicated. Use all feedback to improve.

Sales Pitch: Two major factors which would determine the quality of your leads are using the right platform and the way to pitch the customer. We have seen that there are numerous platforms for lead generation, but one should choose wisely based on the customer profile and audience design. The second part, or the sales pitch, plays a significant role in not only generating the leads, but also ensuring that the leads are of quality. Let's take an example of a sales pitch going wrong, suppose you use email marketing for lead generation, then your email should not be a long essay but rather should be concise and like a magnet using baiting statements. To have great sales pitch it is important to have a blueprint of the pitch and the customer feedback reports.

Make a blueprint of "sales pitch," but keep it flexible enough to mold it in a conversation varying from customer to customer.

So here are the different elements that you need to consider while making your sales pitch:

1. **Overcoming Objections**: Your sales is all about convincing/persuading people to buy something. But a person might not be convinced and you would need to overcome their objections to convince them. Yes, this does sound stereotyped, but we can't forget the basics of sales while formulating our sales pitch. Use feedback to eliminate the objections that are raised previously and keep molding your sales pitch to overcome these objections in an effective way.

2. **Identify and Engage**: The most effective way for businesses to sell is by identifying the needs of their prospective customer, engaging with them, and aligning your offerings with the customer's needs. So don't overwhelm people with sales pitches when they don't want to buy your product, but instead, you should be having an engaging, mutually beneficial conversation with your prospective customers, where you can demonstrate the value of your offer. Engagement leads to great feedback which should be used to improve your sales pitch.

3. **Collaborative approach**: When you are engaging with your prospective customer, you are trying to create a bond or relationship and in turn build a good network. But as a start-up, it might be hard initially to find the right leads, so collaborative efforts are required. So a collaborative approach to sales would mean that you're trying to learn from your customers to improve your product. A sales pitch starts evolving into capture and magnet mode when you are able to find the right balance for what you sell, in a way that it will seemingly benefit your customers more than it costs them to buy from you.

4. **Build credibility**: The best sales relationships are built on trust. Building credibility might include sharing some details about your team, advisors or investors. Or you could build credibility earlier on by being a socially responsible business or environmentally sustainable etc. Your sales pitch should have a trust building part and these stories become a part of your pitch. Your product or service has to fit into a broader context and needs to be trusted and the sales pitch should encompass these attributes.

So make your sales pitch using these four pointers. You must remember that making a sale is not about receiving something on a one-time transactional basis, but it is about giving to your customers to form long-term relationships. Show the customer that you care about them and that you're interested in more than just making a sale.

Start-ups face many challenges, and you probably would have a short roster of existing clients, but sales can get a lot easier if you change your perspective. Learn not to push anyone into buying from you, but instead, let your own natural inclinations and sense of authenticity guide your sales process and help you build relationships and help people along the way.

SALES PROMOTION:

With all information from above, you are geared up for sales. Let me add another element of focus – sales promotion. This would be the decision maker, the tipping over technique that can be used effectively. You offer an incentive designed to persuade your prospective customer to purchase your product or service now rather than later. Sales promotions are usually offered to individual customers, but could also be directed towards businesses. The key purpose of a sales promotion is to create a sense of urgency in a buyer's decision-making, hopefully tipping them over to the "will buy now" side. A sales promotion might be helpful also to induce repeat purchases or referrals.

So, there you have it! A complete guide to your Sales & Marketing Blueprint. Just make sure that your sales and marketing are aligned. As today, a business can only be successful when they've made a commitment to sales and marketing alignment. Have cohesion and make sure your sales and marketing teams feed off each other and ensure sharing knowledge and expertise. Understanding together what it takes to get qualified leads and close sales and you would be on your way to improved performance and greater revenue.

I have added a complete chapter on Digital Marketing after this due to its relevance in today's world and it's ability to reach a global marketplace. You can reach more customers for less amount spent than traditional marketing methods. You could even reach out to more consumers in your target market. Digital Marketing is a strategic tool for businesses and it consists of every single marketing effort a company makes in the digital environment… More in the next chapter.

> *"Success looks a lot like failure up until the moment you break through the finish line."*
>
> *– Dan Waldschmidt*

SALES & MARKETING

SALES PITCH TEMPLATE

Answer the following questions:

CUSTOMER

#1	Who is the target customer:
#2	What is the major customer need:
#3	Major customer demographics:

MARKET

#4	General product/service category:	
#5	Typical competitors:	

PRODUCT/SERVICE

#6	Product/service name:
#7	Major benefits
#8	Major differentiator:

Use your answers to create your sales pitch:

We help _____ (#1, #3) with their _____ (#2) by using _____ (#6). Unlike _____ (#5) who provide _____ (#4), we help our customer by providing _____ (#7). We are able to do that through _____ (#8).

Illustration from peopleplusenterprise.co.uk

Chapter 10
DIGITAL MARKETING

Continuing from the previous chapter on Sales and Marketing, it was important to cover Digital Marketing separately due to its relevance in today's world and it's ability to reach a global marketplace. You can reach more customers for less amount spent than traditional marketing methods. You could even reach out to more consumers in your target market. Digital Marketing is a strategic tool for businesses and it consists of every single marketing effort a company makes in the digital environment.

So what do you as a business owner need for you to be successful in digital marketing? Well, you would need a diverse set of skills and a good knowledge of all digital marketing disciplines and tools. You are going to be promoting your product or service online, so you must have a grasp of all channels available to you. Either learn the art yourself or hire someone to do it for you, either ways it is my recommendation that you are aware of the basic skills and tools in digital marketing.

So, the basic goals in digital marketing for your business should be the following:

- SEO campaigns - Design, implementation & monitoring
- PPC campaigns - Optimization and Analysis

- Content Marketing - Supervise and drive campaigns
- Social Media - Utilize the networks optimally
- Email Marketing - Work on funnels and flow
- Mobile Marketing - Responsive and relevant campaigns
- Analysis: Coordinate activities & analyse the performance of all digital marketing channels

What I am trying to get at is that you do not have to be an expert in all disciplines but it is going to add a lot of value to your business if you have a broad knowledge of how digital marketing works in general and not just a single discipline. I am going to cover all of these segments so at the end of this chapter, you would have a good grasp of the subject.

Image by Darwin Langanzon from Pixabay

So how are you, as a business owner, going to use digital marketing. First, get the concept clear on what you are trying to achieve here. You need to support the marketing and sales team by implementing marketing strategies in the online environment and should align the entire process with the strategic goals of your company. As we saw in sales and marketing, the objective is to listen to the voice of the customer and how they want to interact with a brand digitally. You should be able to have a strategic approach in building digital channels and have integrated content to minimize cost, drive traffic and acquisitions. In the past decade, digital marketing has become a vital component in a company's overall marketing strategy.

The problem with learning these days is that technology changes quickly. Some of the big failed social media platforms include big names like iTunes ping, google wave, Google Orkut, Myspace, Friendster, vine to name a few. They failed and people moved on to what they liked better. The hot social media platform of today may be all but forgotten by next year. So you have to equip yourself with the fundamentals as most of the foundational principles of digital marketing remain the same. You just need to know where the customers are and be attuned to the changes in technology, social media and software platforms.

The basics of marketing have not changed since the days when businesses mainly advertised in print, radio and TV. You still would need strong communication skills and a strong base in marketing principles, all you need to do is adapt the same to the online world. Data, existing or new, becomes very important. Technology has helped us with great tools at our disposal to be able to capture the market today. You have tools like Google Analytics, HubSpot, Hootsuite, Mailchimp, Clickfunnels, etc. that make life much easier for your business. Ads have become very targeted and you can choose the audience and the demographic you want to show your ad to, be it Facebook, Google, Instagram or LinkedIn. Content marketing has really grown and It allows businesses to tailor messages for a specific audience, and market directly to people who are likely to be interested in their product or service.

I think of digital marketing strategy for a business to be all about getting found, getting noticed, getting leads, and then turning those leads into a sale, with getting returning customers and referrals as a big bonus. You have to be aligned to your bigger marketing strategy and try to communicate your marketing message to a target audience on the right platform and with the right pitch, else the messages will not be received in the way in which we intended. Since digital marketing is a rapidly changing space and it is imperative for businesses to keep themselves up to date on new tools and emerging platforms. It all comes down to competition and staying ahead of it. The landscape for businesses is changing so rapidly, that it has become a necessity to keep a step ahead of the competition, learn from their successful strategies and of course their mistakes. Do keep competition analysis to help you form a better digital strategy.

Tool 17: Seven pillars of Digital Marketing

So, let's jump into it. Digital marketing can be broadly segmented into 7 main categories as I had mentioned above, at the start, as the goals for your business, namely: Search Engine Optimization, Pay-per-Click, Social Media Marketing, Content Marketing, Email Marketing, Mobile Marketing, and Marketing Analytics.

SEARCH ENGINE OPTIMIZATION (SEO)

The main aim of search engine optimization (SEO), is to get your business to rank higher in search results, these days mostly on Google, as other search engines like Bing or Baidu don't even come close to the 75% market share that Google enjoys. You need to ideally have a website and should be trying to increase search engine traffic to the website. To achieve this, research words and phrases people are using to search for information online, and use those words and phrases in your own content. It's important to understand that SEO is very challenging because your success of higher ranking or improvement of search ranking position always depends on Google and its most current algorithm. Google is known to keep changing and tweaking its algorithm, so you have to be updated and changing your SEO strategy along with Google.

There are many ways to boost your site's organic rankings. You could improve your title tag, know your highest-level category pages, use keyword planners from Google themselves, learn from what keywords are working for your competition, optimize your website, work on new and regular content and have a social media network of platforms. What I am going to do is explain the three most basic fundamentals of SEO relevant for any business and with any algorithm that Google develops.

Content indexing: You need to improve your indexing like adding alt text for images and adding text transcripts for video or audio content. This needs to be done to ensure that search engines are able to read clearly what your site content is. Google themselves provide some of the best tools available. The easiest to use and probably the fastest is the URL Inspection tool by Google.

Good link structure: Crawling is basically the discovery process in which search engines send out a team of crawlers to find new and updated content. It may be any type of content or format, it is discovered by links. So it is important that search engines can easily crawl your site structure, to find the content on your site. It is good to use sitemaps, which is the simplest, fastest way to get your URLs indexed. The tool you could use for this is the Search Console Sitemap Report, where you could submit sitemaps.

Keywords and keyword targeting: One of the fundamental building blocks of SEO is to be able to properly deploy your keywords, which are basically the search terms you want in your content and headers of your website. Now it has become more targeted and technical, so you can't just fill your content with as many keywords and keyword variations as possible. Now it is better to write quality content that uses keywords in the headers and also mentions them in the page content, which is crawlable, and will make pages rank better in search results. Google's own Keyword Planner and Ahref's Keyword Explorer are some of the best tools you could use.

PAY-PER-CLICK (PPC)

Pay-per-click(PPC) is an online advertising system where the advertisers have to pay each time a user clicks on one of their online ads. There are different types of PPC ads, but the paid search ad is the most common. The search engine that dominates is again Google as almost three-quarters of people searching online are using Google. PPC works especially when people are looking for something to buy, like a commercial search, so in all such cases PPC model of paid advertisements and promoted search engine results really comes in handy. Once you are no longer paying, your ad will cease to exist, so PPC works only for a short-term. Like SEO, PPC is a way to drive search traffic to your business online. One of the things that differentiate PPC from SEO is that you only pay for the results.

So where do you see these ads? Remember the advertisements you see at the top and sides of a page when you search and get results, the ads you see when you are simply browsing the web, ads before those YouTube videos or the pesky ads in mobile applications, all these are examples of PPC ads. As Google dominates the space, one of the main tools or a typical PPC model is the Google AdWords campaign, in which you will pay Google only when someone clicks on your ad and lands on your online platform like website, landing page, etc. The amount you spend on PPC can vary based on your advertising budgets, but success is not guaranteed and the budgets alone do not determine the quality of results.

Competition for keywords and space also plays an important part on how much you end up paying. What it costs to run an ad or promote your search results depends primarily on how much competition there is for the keywords you have selected. Keywords that have higher competition, like the keywords that are searched for by many people, are the ones that most websites or landing pages would like to be found for. Therefore, these keywords having high competition will be more expensive, which conversely means that the lower competition keywords and terms will likely cost less.

SERP is the term given to the Search Engine Results Page. For your ads, as an advertiser, to appear alongside the results on a search engine, you cannot just pay more to make your ads more prominent than your competitor's ads. You have to take part in an auction, known as the Ad Auction, which is an automated process that search engines like Google use to determine the validity and the relevance of advertisements. The Ad Auction is a bidding system which means that you must bid on the keywords and key terms you want to be searched for, so that your ads are displayed.

You need to set up pay-per-click ad campaigns, depending upon geographic areas. You will be able to choose whether your ad is displayed to users all over the world, or only within a specific geographic area. Knowing who you need to target and being specific in your selection of areas helps you reduce cost. There are many tools available these days for an effective PPC ad campaign. I have already mentioned the Google Keyword Planner, but do check out tools like SEMrush, Wordstream, Adwords, Performance and Ispionage. For Amazon try to use tools like PPC Entourage or Ad Badger.

SOCIAL MEDIA MARKETING (SMM)

Social media marketing or SMM is probably the most influential and powerful pillar of Digital Marketing today. We all know that the social media is a fast-growing trend and has even grown faster than the internet. What we do not realize is that social media platforms are not only used for social networking but are also a great way to digitally advertise your products and services. That it works for any size of a business is a plus. You need to be able to speak directly with your targeted audiences social platforms like Facebook, Twitter, Instagram, Pinterest, Reddit etc. Digital marketing on social media can create buzz for your brand, drive leads, sales which overall brings amazing success to your business.

SMM in my books ranks higher as it reaches out to your target audience at a more effective rate. It is important to use platforms that are regularly used by your potential customers and where most users relevant to you spend a larger chunk of their time during the day or night. If you are looking for good leads through SMM, you need to make the most out of these customer's habits. Engagement is good, but social media advertisements are better. You have to realize that you would reach a large number of people the moment you post an ad, which helps you reduce your costs. Your SMM should be aligned to your other marketing functions. The message and brand narrative that you project must be similar and coordinated across all platforms, online and off, so that every part of the brand is telling the same story.

So, SMM would include everything your business does via social media platforms. You must approach SMM with an integrated and strategic approach. It is not just about creating posts and responding to comments. Your posts have to be consistent, coordinated and you could use a lot of these online tools available to automate and schedule social media posts, while monitoring and engaging manually. One of the most crucial parts of SMM would be analytics. You have to be able to analyze the performance of your posts, and then based on the data you get, rejig your strategy.

SMM is going to be a wee-bit more complicated than managing your personal Facebook or Twitter profile or page. So let me help you with the required blend of creative thinking and objective, data-driven strategy, which might be a great fit for you. Do these Five steps and your SMM strategy would be set:

Step 1: Content Planning: Build a SMM marketing plan. Then start building your content. Content is the most important element of social media marketing. The content includes your images, videos, info graphics, teasers, guides, reels, etc. For brainstorming content ideas use keyword research, look at trends, look at competition, always keeping the interests of your target audience as a guiding principle. Just make sure you post regularly and make that content helpful and interesting for your potential customers.

Step 2: Consistent Brand Image: Your business's core identity, be it reliability, responsibility, trustworthy or fun, should always stay consistent. Every channel has its own unique environment, so there has to be a uniform approach in delivering content to the variety of different social media platforms. When your target audience is being presented with your core messaging and other brand elements repeatedly, it helps tremendously in brand recognition. So, step 2 is to ensure consistency of your brand messaging in line with your values, identity and strategy.

Step 3: Context: We have to be working on seeking attention of our target audience for each of our new content on each of our chosen social media platforms, so context is very important to understand. There are ways to get attention, like emotions, setting, story, but you also have to consider how the specific platform or ad type is tuned to attention. It's no longer enough to simply be in the feed. Twitter would be relevant for delivery of shorter posts while a blog post would be used by your readers for detailed information or motivation.

Step 4: Promotion and Hashtags: You need to be able to choose the channels where your target audience is more represented, find the most appropriate ways of communication and then effectively influence your target audience. Curated content, shares and hashtags are very important for effective promotion. Twitter, Facebook, Instagram, and Pinterest all use shares and hashtags aligned your content with the current trends. This assists promotion as your content becomes easier for users to discover and therefore it would be more likely that they'll share it.

Step 5: Analytics: A key part of your SMM strategy should be analytics and tracking data. Tools like Facebook Pixel and Google Analytics are provided free of cost to enable you to mine tremendous amount of data and insights on the performance of you campaigns. You would be able to measure your most effective ads, audiences, techniques, as well as allow you to abandon the ones that don't work. All your SMM campaigns on each social media platform you use, should be properly monitored, for insight into which of your content and context is performing best with your audience.

You would have got the gist that social media is a very powerful platform which you cannot ignore in this digital era. Just be focused on having an influential social media presence and create attractive, persuasive and appealing content, that would connect to your target audience instantly.

Image by Gerd Altmann from Pixabay

CONTENT MARKETING

Content marketing is like a mutually beneficial relationship with other forms of digital marketing. You use all elements of digital marketing like incorporating SEO search terms into website content, share the content created as social media posts using SMM, then expand your reach through email marketing publications etc. You are basically trying to increase brand awareness by using simple but useful storytelling styles and sharing information. Acquisition of the target audience is the key here, like them requesting more information, signing up for a newsletter or an email list, or making a transaction. Content could be a blog post, podcasts, videos, white papers, e-books, etc. Try not to just advertise your product or service or try to make a sale, but also look at creating and providing value for your consumer.

Content marketing is about building a trustworthy, continuous and feasible relationship with your potential customers. You should work on a long term association with your customer in mind and not just making a single sale, and be rest assured that association would lead to many sales and referrals over time. Long term association goals need to be built with trust and reliability as the foundation, so you should always be offering readers informative and useful material that provides them insights and value.

Start by building a content library. As I mentioned before, content marketing is a long-term strategy. So you need to build a library of your content and list them according to the category like text, video, podcast, etc. This content library will help you organizing your resources for brand awareness and would assist you in building your profile as an information resource, that will continue to bring users to your site via search engines. When people do visit your platform for information, ideally they will relate to you as an authority on the subject and this helps when they are going to make a purchase.

As always, analytics play a key role and data tells you a lot about your customers and what are they looking for when they interact with you. Monitor data to determine what content works and what does not generate interest. Some of the key metrics you can monitor are organic traffic and conversions, keyword rankings, bounce rate, time spent on a page, new users etc. The ultimate goal of your content marketing strategy should be to increase brand awareness and induce conversation around what you have to offer.

Email Marketing

The past decade has seen an emergence and tremendous growth of social media, mobile applications and various other channels, but if you are still looking at the most effective marketing techniques, it is still the good old Email. Email marketing is a vibrant and robust way to connect with your target audience. You could use emails as a part of your content marketing strategy, providing value, information, and over time convert an audience into paying customers. Customer acquisitions is the key goal and email marketing is the path you should choose for converting people into members, customers or supporters.

There are many reasons that come to mind as to why you should choose Email marketing. On a direct comparison with social media marketing, it has been surprisingly found that while social media is a great channel for interacting with your audience and strengthening your personal relationships with them, the more effective medium for customer acquisition was emails, compared to social media. For small business owners too email marketing is found to be very cost effective, easy and effective, wherein you could reach a large target audience at a very minimal per message cost. It can be personalized and customized for a tailored audience. Email is transactional by nature and one could reply, forward, link, sign-up, or maybe buy just with email. It is device agnostic and you are using emails on smartphones, laptops, tablets, pc, mac or watches.

To get the most out of email marketing, I suggest using an automated tool. Luckily for you, there are so many free email marketing tools available which could be used to send kickback emails from lead offers, thank you emails, promotion, create stunning newsletters, campaigns and so much more. Top of the list of suggestions for free tools are Hubspot, Sender, Sendinblue and Mailchimp. You could definitely do a simple google search here to compare and use the most suitable. I personally use 3-4 tools sometimes so you don't have to be married to one tool. And who knows, by the time this book gets printed, some more great new tools might be available. Simple, use automation tools for email marketing.

To top everything, email marketing is one of the most measurable marketing tools available to you for analytics. You can track everything from opens, clicks, location, conversion, bounce rate, etc. The most important still remain the open rate and the click through rate. So to get more opens and click through, there are a few tricks that you could deploy to make your emails more appealing to users and more likely to be opened. These include:

Creating a Sense of Urgency: This is a play on an old time-share marketing gimmick wherein they would create a perception that time is running out to get a special deal or that there are only a limited numbers available. It really works in emails too and a perception of missing out can increase the number of people clicking through on your links.

Personalizing Email: This is the real power of emails, personalization. Using simple tricks like incorporating the recipient's name is a proven way to increase open and click through rates. This can be achieved with minimal effort with the proper automation tools I mentioned before.

Preferences for trust: You need to be able to build trust with your emails so that you are not considered spam. So allow recipients to specify how often they want to hear from you, whether they do not want any more emails and unsubscribe from your list, etc.

So be ready to use email marketing to create compelling campaigns, have an optimal audience outreach, analyze your interactions and data, and make strategic decisions based on that data.

Mobile Marketing

In the last few years, ever since the advent of the real efficient smart phone capable of handling faster processing like a desktop, customers have started to shift their attention to mobile. This digital marketing type is primarily focused on reaching your target audience through their smart phone or tablet. Mobile marketing reaches people through text messages, social media, websites, email and mobile applications. Everyone today is on the go, so on their portable smart devices they require personalized, time and location-based information so that they can get what they want and when they want it. Slowly and steadily mobile is becoming the future of marketing.

Like other digital marketing pillars, mobile marketing also involves advertising that appear on mobile devices. Ad formats, styles, concepts and customization vary based on the platform, as most platforms offer their own distinctive ad options. What's more, mobile marketing ads will help you to reach a larger audience. And if you want your audience to be able to reach you through their mobile devices, make sure you focus on having a mobile friendly website.

To succeed in mobile marketing you need three elements:

- Mobile friendly content
- Use of mobile applications and platforms
- Create effective mobile advertising with target audience in mind

Also, the different types of strategies for mobile marketing are:

- App based marketing
- QR codes
- SMS and push notification
- In game marketing
- Location based marketing'
- Search through mobile
- Coupons
- Payments
- VR/AR

Mobile marketing is definitely useful to reach a wider audience. Message delivery can be a lot more personalized and effective, due to the fact that mobile marketing is location-based. Some of the other benefits of mobile marketing are that it is easy to track, you can target a specific group of people, go viral, benefit your search engine rankings, is cost-effective and you can have a fast and real-time communication with your audience to gain quick results.

Marketing Analytics

We have gone through six different pillars of digital marketing. In almost every type of strategy I have written about, I have emphasized the importance of analytics. This is because the biggest advantage using digital marketing is that it can be tracked and measured. I still remember the days of the coupons and when Groupon became big, that was the only traceable marketing option. But analytics has completely evolved and changed today. We have such awesome tools at our disposal which can track user behavior and its minutest details like link-clicks, time spent on a web page, traffic, open rates, bounce rates etc. There is just an enormous amount of information and data available and your endeavor should be to understand and then strategize based on inputs you receive.

You are going to need digital marketing analytics if you are to build an online presence that helps to promote your brand and business. Data is the key here, and the study of data gives you optimal results in your marketing efforts, so it is imperative that you are able to evaluate and understand the data, and then build a strategy around it. Insights into your marketing initiatives and their performance allows you the maneuverability to alter strategies or tactics. Your marketing message should resonate with your potential customers and analytics allows you to learn what messaging is successful with them.

Luckily for us, there are many tools available, the best surprisingly free as they are provided by the companies themselves, as they want your ad money and assist you with providing analytics for better efficiency. The tools are used for measuring the success of your digital marketing campaigns, and you could use a combination of these tools, depending on your requirements and your audience. My favorite tool for website analytics is Google Analytics. Google has provided this free tool which you can customize to your liking and preferences to give you unquestionably the best insights and measurements on hundreds of parameters like how your site is performing, which keywords are acquiring, navigation through your website, bounce rates and much more. You also get real time data in Google analytics, which makes it very dynamic. The other great free tool is Facebook Pixel. With Instagram and WhatsApp acquired, Facebook is becoming a force to reckon with in the digital space, and the pixel tool has great insights and data that can be mined. Over time, you won't just be using analytics to measure your campaigns but surely analytics will also allow you to improve your campaigns.

There you have it, a whole chapter on digital marketing and I still have loads that I can write. It is such a vast subject matter, and definitely evolving with time. Traditional marketing has taken a little step back and we all have to change with the times and embrace the new king of marketing. Digital marketing has kind of become the new normal for a successful business, so you definitely need to be on board to grow your business. Embrace the opportunity, get more sales, increase your profit. Good luck!

> *"Marketing is no longer about the stuff that you make, but about the stories you tell."*
>
> *– Seth Godin*

Chapter 11

PROTECT YOUR BUSINESS & IP

> *"People recognize intellectual property the same way they recognize real estate. People understand what property is. But it's a new kind of property, and so the understanding uses new control surfaces. It uses a new way of defining the property."*
>
> *– Michael Nesmith*

I have previously written about protecting your intellectual property, brand and protecting your ideas. In today's business landscape, protection is essential to growing your business. Infringers are everywhere and looking to capture a piece of the success pie that you have created, so it is necessary for you to be able to deter them from disrupting your business and shield your business with security in the event of attempted infringement. So, you need to have a complete strategy to protect your business and it's interests. I will walk you through a strategy that's traditionally been considered a defensive business strategy, but I actually perceive it as an offensive business strategy. I'll put it out there and you decide the defensive or the offensive nature of the plan.

STARTUP... JUST STARTUP

Once upon a time, there was a castle. Lol, don't get alarmed, I am not going to tell a story. The castle is just for you to picture a structure with a moat around it like in medieval times and that's what I am suggesting you do for your business. You have to create a moat around your business. If you're not familiar with what a moat is, it is this little lake like water body around a fortification to protect and add to the defence. So using the same analogy, I would like you to create an economic moat around your business. Warren Buffet made the term "economic moat" very popular and always talked about the ability of a business to maintain a competitive advantage over its competitors, to protect its longer-term profits and market share. But how would you create this economic moat for your business? And where is the attack in all this defence talk?

Well, this kind of defence and creation of a barrier for competition is part of my defensive attacking strategy. First defend, then attack. Because when you've become successful everyone is going to try and copy your success model. So not only you have to protect your success, you have to ensure you out succeed everyone and run away from your competition. Keeping the competition at bay is the defence, leaving them behind is the attack. Don't be naïve to think what you have cannot be copied. Everything can be copied or rebuilt, just takes a reasonable amount of time, adequate resources and the right personnel. Like for example, it only takes an efficient software development team to build the core features of Facebook, Uber, AirBnB or any other billion-dollar businesses.

Yup, building or rebuilding that software is not the problem, that is just a small barrier and good teams can build it easily. What is difficult and the actual mountain barrier is the creation of users. Facebook has like say a billion plus users and they have users posting their personal content on the platform, interactions, friends, networks, all making Facebook a behemoth with a barrier very difficult to climb. It is easy for someone to build a software just like Facebook, but how do you build the users and the experiences?

So, by now you are understanding my concept of a moat. the key is to create value and then with that value you create a barrier to entry. Once you have a barrier that others are unable to breach you start strengthening your model and customizations so that you leave the competition far behind. And the reason I say that it's a defensive attacking strategy is that you have to go on the attack and out-compete and outgrow your competition. Your goal shouldn't be to just to protect, defend or even hide, it should be to run away from the competition and out-compete them. That's my preferred way of doing business and that's the way adopted by most businesses, especially technology companies. Ingrain this in your system – you will be successful and you will grow, well, you might as well just grow successful faster and better.

I'm going to digress a little and give you a little insight into what kind of businesses multiply many folds and how you can build one for yourself. Let's start with these brokering platforms. What that means is bringing people together. Building communities. Could be something like dating sites, meetups, socializing, whiskey clubs, art clubs, book clubs etc. Bring people together and the day you have built a community, you have a winner. Another expandable business idea is to bring together buyers and sellers, for example, Amazon. More ideas coming to my mind, bring together creators and consumers of content like YouTube. Make course content intensive sites like Udemy bringing knowledge givers and receivers together. The idea behind all these businesses and their success is the ability to create a Critical Mass, after which it's incredibly difficult to catch up to them (moat-defence) and then these just grow because their brand recognition increases (attack) after the critical mass is achieved. The magic of critical mass is when a lot of people use your product or service, a lot of people discuss and a lot of them refer.

I used the example of Udemy. Let me use it to explain my point better. Let's say there is someone on Udemy who has managed to reach critical mass i.e., grown their user base and created a course that is highly reviewed, positively. This person taught a software, say Blender. For anyone searching for a course on Blender on the Udemy platform, they first see this one person with a moat. His course is a moat because he's got 30000 reviews and mostly positive. The next best person has 4000 reviews, which for me, is in itself a moat, but when you compare it to the 30000, it seems overshadowed. Now the next person and all others have less than 400 reviews. My question to you is, who would you select when you want to learn Blender? Most of you, including me will probably choose based on reviews and experiences and if 30,000 people recommend a person, I would be automatically biased and convinced enough to select the person with the highest approval rating. The person on Udemy had a critical mass and now his business feeds off this. Create the critical mass people, and the growth is inevitable! The critical mass is the moat and the growth.

Image by Gordon Johnson from Pixabay

> *"A wise man will always allow a fool to rob him of ideas without yelling "Thief."*
> *If he is wise he has not been impoverished.*
> *Nor has the fool been enriched.*
> *The thief flatters us by stealing.*
> *We flatter him by complaining."*
>
> – Ben Hecht, A Child of the Century

Don't let the mindset be too defensive when forming a strategy for your business. You definitely have to be on the offensive, attack and be really aggressive. It is the most effective methodology and counter-productive to the purely defensive strategies. I have been talking about a moat and a barrier to entry you need to create, but what happens when you yourself are a first time entrepreneur? You end up on the wrong side of the moat and are actually facing it rather than creating it. This is the challenge most start-ups face when they enter the markets, there is some other company who has made a huge barrier to entry and has a critical mass. This is what I have to help you overcome. Let's face the truth, the market is going to be very difficult and the competition is intense and formidable. Another issue is that most first-time entrepreneurs lack resources. So, what is the solution? Specialization and creating a niche.

Tool 18: Specialization and creating a niche:

Specialization in business involves focusing on a limited scope of products or services so as to become more efficient. Focus and creating a niche for your business is the key take away. You can easily increase the productivity of your business and give it the necessary competitive advantage. Specialization, for me, could be a great way of accelerating growth of your business. It all again comes down to the value that is created for your clients and the differentiation, but don't try to be different for difference's sake. It is easy to be different on paper, like writing on your website that you're the best at so and so, but remember that, especially in service businesses, customers are the judge and jury. They would decide not just by what you say about yourself, but about how you perform and meet the expectations set. Customer experience and interaction becomes the key. So, yes, specialize and differentiate, but do it well and deliver on expectations.

Specialization itself can be categorized. There are typically two different types of specialization, Vertical and Horizontal. Let me briefly give you an idea of what these both are about:

a. **Vertical Specialization**: This is when you focus on a particular type of client, in a particular industry or niche.

b. **Horizontal Specialization**: this is when you focus on a specific problem or solution, agnostic to the industries and sectors.

Specialization can be really valuable for a number of reasons. First, it makes it easier to choose for your customers. Let's say there is a car sales company, and they're looking for sales training for their staff, then given the choice between a generic sales trainer and a specialist sales trainer in automotive sales, they're probably going to pick the specialist, all other aspects being equal. When you specialize, you also develop expertise much more quickly, certainly much quicker than people who are spreading their experience more thinly across different fields.

If you're regularly working in the same industry or on the same problem consistently, you are definitely going to develop a lot of experience and expertise in that particular area. I knew a guy who only customized and repaired Ferraris and though he had a small market segment, he got a lot of business and repeat business as word spread that he was a specialist. Specialization, if done right, can be a really powerful tool to gain that critical mass and build a moat around your business.

CREATING A NICHE:

We know that we are going to face competition. Trying to launch and grow a business in a market filled with competitors can be tough. One way to stand out from the competition is by focusing on a niche market. A niche market is basically a focused target audience that requires a specific product or service. Identifying the needs of a niche market can be an effective way to come up with a business idea for a successful product or service. I have always been focused on a smaller specialized market as trying to break into a large marketplace initially can be very difficult. When you have scores of competitors all vying for the same customers, it's tough to gain brand loyalty, especially if those competitors are large corporations that have built a critical mass and a moat through a strong customer base.

Creating a niche in the market and making it the start of your business strategy, on the other hand, can give you more freedom for trial and error, more flexibility and you can limit the resources accordingly. Your chances improve for capturing your audience and winning their business when you have fewer competitors to work against. Your approach then becomes more customized and personal for the consumers of your product or service. With an abundance of specialized resources, tools and online platforms, identifying and reaching a target audience has never been easier for small business owners. Let me help you further by giving you the right tools to make your niche business a hit.

a. *Create a Simple Service*

Define a narrow customer base. Go back to my chapter on customer journey blueprint if you need pointers. Then create a limited offering that focuses on the needs of your defined customer base. I used to watch a lot of shark tank, and you would be surprised at the success of brands like Tipsy Elves, Scrub Daddy and

Squatty Potty, but it clearly shows the success of a simple focused products. When you are planning, just make sure you are aware of who needs your product or service, what's uniquely useful about it that makes it better than your competition. Then just fine-tune your strategy to focus solely on selling your unique specialization and expertise.

b. *Build Your Niche Marketplace*

Once you have created your simple service it is time to take advantage on a niche marketplace that you feel is being underserved. As I had defined earlier, a niche marketplace is a specialized, small market segment within a larger, feasible commercial industry. What you are looking to do is to understand the demographics of your small segment and why the customers are underserved. Once we know this we just have to unite them and serve them better. They have a problem and you need to find a simple solution to their problem. As you have learnt in this book earlier, create a buyer's persona and a detailed profile of your target customer. Collect data and use it to connect with your niche marketplace. Reach out to the interested people, decision makers and even influencers.

c. *Expertise*

Now you have a simple product or service and your niche marketplace. Now is the time to kick it up a notch, and you do that by offering valuable insight and advice. However, you cannot simply proclaim that you are an expert. You have to be authentic and build credibility. Understanding the needs of your customer and interacting with them is what is going to help your business. Be willing to tell the story behind the foundation of your product or service, personalize the interaction. Learn so much about your small focused business and your marketplace that you start being the leading authority in it. Write blogs, newsletters, reach out, give seminars, network. Once you establish yourself as the leading authority and people start referring to, talking about it, that is when you start building the critical mass and the moat around your business. It is a process, be authentic, be learned and be positive.

d. *USP and Relevance*

Every business should have a unique selling point that makes you stand apart from the competition. Hammer away that point strongly and seize every opportunity to point out why your product or service is a better offer for your niche marketplace than your competitors and their offerings. So knowing your USP is very important. It makes you stand out. Keep in mind that the offering and the USP should be relevant to your niche marketplace. Don't be a multi-service one-stop-shop, rather be a specialist, an expert and you will find out that people prefer that. If you have a USP and are relevant, then the price you command can be adjusted higher accordingly and you would not have to compete on lower price points.

e. *Repeat the success*

Success is sweet. Once you have the formula for success you have to keep hammering your message home. That does not mean you stop innovating and finding new ways to grow your business. It means that you need to expand on your successes. Repeat the success formula, create a healthy word of mouth and then everything extrapolates. The whole point about being in a specialized and niche market place is to be able to compete on your strengths and increase your exposure.

BARRIERS TO ENTRY:

While we have discussed creation of a moat and critical mass, we are moving towards creation of barriers of entry. Barriers to entry, are all the factors that prevent and limit your competition from entering your market. There are mainly four types of barriers to entry that you could create –

i. Legal: this includes your patents, licenses, copyrights etc.

ii. Technical: this would be the monopoly, high start-up costs, technical know-how, expertise, etc.)

iii. Strategic: example would be disruptive pricing, first mover advantage, etc.

iv. Brand loyalty: this is difficult to create and happens over time and needs authenticity and delivery of expectations from your end.

Tool 19: Protect your Intellectual Property

Innovation in ideas, products, service and strategies is key to a start-up and an entrepreneur. To foster this innovation, it is critical for you to protect your intellectual property. Research and development thrive, and innovations happen because there are laws that protect ideas, allowing businesses or individuals to reap the full benefits of their inventions. If you are an artist, and you are not fully compensated for your content creations, then this would hamper the viability of your art.

Image by Pete Linforth from Pixabay

Intellectual Property (IP) protection is the legal protection of intangible assets such as copyrights, patents, trademarks, unique concepts, and ideas, just as the tangible property. IP would be ownership of one's ideas and it is because of IP that creating a unique product for your business or bringing innovative ideas into reality can prove to be a priceless asset. Newer entrepreneurs, at least a majority of them, don't recognize the need of protecting their IP. Even the ones who are aware, don't really know where to start, so let me categorize the different types of intellectual properties.

COPYRIGHT:

Copyright is a legal term used to describe the rights that creators have over their literary and artistic works. Works covered by copyright range from books, music, videos, paintings, images, sculpture and films, to computer programs, databases, advertisements, maps and technical drawings. You can defend your copyright and even platforms like YouTube do it for me. All images used in this book are free for commercial use through Pixabay, but I have still given the credit under the images to the owners of copyrights of the images. You must respect the work of others and give them their due.

PATENTS:

A patent is an exclusive right granted for an invention. Generally speaking, a patent provides the patent owner with the right to decide whether the invention can be used by others and how it can be used. In exchange for this right, the patent owner makes technical information about the invention publicly available in the published patent document. I must warn you though that patents are very expensive and time-consuming. Also, you would require different patents in different geographical regions. So think about getting a patent only if you feel you really have some innovation or tech that need protection. Even with a patent, people make small adjustments in their copies and you suffer as you have spent a bomb on the patents. Think twice before patents.

TRADEMARKS:

A trademark is a sign that distinguishes the goods or services of one business from those of other businesses. I suggest, you must trademark your brand. Trademarks are used since long and big corporate like McDonalds, Coke, Starbucks, Nike, etc. live by them and protect their trademark rights. To strongly discourage copies and similar sounding brand poaching like McRonalds, Coco Cola, Stanbucks, Nikey etc.

INDUSTRIAL DESIGNS:

An industrial design constitutes the appearance or aesthetic aspect of a product. A design may consist of three-dimensional features, such as the shape or surface of a product, or of two-dimensional features, such as patterns, lines or color. In principle, an industrial design right does not protect the technical or functional features of a product.

Geographical Indications:

Geographical indications or GIs identify a good as originating from a particular place. By contrast, a trademark identifies a good or service as originating from a particular company. Geographical indications and appellations of origin are signs used on goods that have a specific geographical origin and possess qualities, a reputation or characteristics that are essentially attributable to that place of origin. Most commonly, a geographical indication includes the name of the place of origin of the goods. Tequila is a good example and is associated with the agave plants from Mexico.

Trade Secrets:

Trade secrets are intellectual property rights on confidential information which may be licensed or even sold. The unauthorized acquisition, use or disclosure of such secret information in a manner contrary to honest commercial practices by others is regarded as an unfair practice and a violation of the trade secret protection.

Non-disclosure Agreement:

Coming to the end of the chapter and going into the final chapter on raising funds (kachhiing!), I want to talk about a document every entrepreneur and business should use, a Non-Disclosure Agreement. You have to maintain a level of secrecy when it comes to research, development, working projects, innovative ideas, or potentially successful new products. This is done to maintain a competitive advantage and the secrecy part is to ensure your info does not fall into the hands of a competitor. Start-ups with an innovative and profitable idea can only succeed if what they are working on remains under wraps. A non-disclosure agreement, or NDA, is a legal document that keeps such sensitive information protected. These agreements may be referred to alternatively as confidentiality agreements, statements, or clauses, within a larger legal document.

An NDA, typically comes into relevance any time your confidential information is disclosed to potential investors, creditors, clients, suppliers or any other entity. Deterrence is the goal here and having confidentiality in writing and signed by all parties can lend trust to negotiations and discussions. The exact nature of the confidential information that needs protection can be explained clearly in the non-disclosure agreement. You can use the NDA to restrict an entity to secrecy so that the signatory does not divulge the confidential information contained in the agreement.

One last point to note, always consult an attorney and take their guidance for legal protection of your ideas, innovations, effort, creations and intellectual property.

Please use an attorney. And keep in mind laws vary from country to country and from state to state even. So, you've got to use a local attorney who understands the law in your area. So remember that it is important to hire a local intellectual property lawyer to deal with your legal rights concerning intellectual and creative innovations and works. A lawyer of intellectual property would defend you in multiple areas including copyrights, patents, trademarks, industrial design rights, duplication, or infringement, trade dress, trade secret and plant variety rights among many others.

> "Intellectual property, more than ever, is a line drawn around information, which asserts that despite having been set loose in the world - and having, inevitably, been created out of an individual's relationship with the world - that information retains some connection with its author that allows that person some control over how it is replicated and used."
> – Nick Harkaway, *The Blind Giant*

Chapter 12

FUNDRAISING

> *"The best entrepreneurs are not the best visionaries. The greatest entrepreneurs are incredible sales people. They know how to tell an amazing story that will convince talent and investors to join in on the journey."*
>
> – Alejandro Cremades, The Art of Startup Fundraising

Kachhing! Money makes a beautiful sound. The problem is that it is not easy to come by. I know this for sure that almost all first-time entrepreneurs struggle financially and almost all entrepreneurs, at some point in their journey, try to raise money in some form. The single most cause of stress for an entrepreneur is the lack of financial stability and thus seeking financial support becomes very important. I am going to outline for you the many different options for raising money. I am not saying that it is imperative to use these options, but just in case you are in the market and have a requirement for funds, then do explore these options. The best strategy is to use a combination of a couple of fund raising options which gets you your desired amount necessary for keeping afloat and grow.

FUNDRAISING

Image by Arek Socha from Pixabay

Tool 20: Funding Options

Every start-up or business entity is unique and different. When it comes to funds, when you require funding and how much you require will be largely dependent on the nature, type and stage of the business. The industry you are in would also determine the premium factor you could command. When you do require the funds, you need to be using the right and the most suitable option for your unique business. To make it easier for you I have listed five funding options that will help you raise capital for your business.

1. **Bootstrapping:**

   Bootstrapping is basically self-funding. When you are just starting your business, then bootstrapping is the most effective way. I have been an investor and one thing I have always looked for is "skin in the game". Bootstrapped startups show that the entrepreneur is fully committed and believes in his product and service so much that he is willing to put his own funds to finance it. It builds faith and authenticity. Furthermore, traction and a definite path for growth is normally required by most investors and you would have trouble getting funding without first showing the goods. You can invest from your own savings or can get your family and friends to contribute. There would be a lot less formalities and compliances to worry about, the cost of raising would be less, the transaction would be easier with a lot of flexibility. Bootstrapping is only suitable when the requirements, initial or otherwise, are small. It is the best option to start with, but then you do have to start looking at the other options of raising funds as and your requirements grow. Stretch your resources as far as you can.

2. **Debt: Bank or NBFI Loans**:

    Normally, Debt is the first thing that comes to mind for a business owner when they start looking for funding. We all are used to the debt model as we have been using it all our lives through student loans, home loans, car loans, etc. So it is natural for an entrepreneur to immediately first think of debt as the best option for raising funds. The Banks and NBFIs (Non-Banking Financial Institutions) provide two kinds of financing for businesses. One is a working capital loan, and the other is funding. Working Capital loan is the loan required to run one complete cycle of revenue generating operations, and the limit is dependent on hypothecating assets. You would of course have to share your business plan, project reports, audited valuation and balance sheets etc. based on which the loan is sanctioned. There are a lot of NBFIs into peer-to-peer lending models these days, which you could check out. Some popular peer-to-peer lending platforms are Upstart, Peerform, Prosper, Funding Circle, etc.

3. **Crowdfunding**:

    Crowdfunding is one of the exciting ways of funding a startup. The concept of crowdfunding is to get contribution, investments, pre-order, like a loan from multiple individuals at the same time. There is a lot of buzz these days on crowdfunding and it has gained a lot of popularity lately. It isn't as easy as it sounds. You have to put up a detailed description of your business, product, service on a crowdfunding platform. Everything needs to be defined clearly, like goals, profit plans, funding requirements and reasons, etc. You only get funding if the people like the idea. Those giving money will make pledges online like pre-buying the product or giving a contribution. If anyone believes in your business and model, they can contribute money towards helping your business. The best thing about crowd funding is that, apart from the financing aspect, it can also generate interest and hence helps in marketing the product. It is also a great way to test the interest levels for your product or service. That being said crowdfunding is a competitive place to earn funding, so make sure your business is solid and can attract the average consumers. Some popular crowdfunding sites are Kickstarter, RocketHub, Dreamfunded, Onevest and GoFundMe.

4. **Angel Investment:**

   Guess what? I have been an Angel Investor and have made a few investments of my own in the startups I believed in. I like the word "angel" investors. Angel investors are basically individuals with money to invest and a keen interest to invest in upcoming start-ups. I have always worked along with networking groups and believe most angel investors work in groups of networks to collectively screen the proposals and do due diligence before investing. This is because you can feed off the expertise of others and that really helps in the decision-making. Clichéd but true, angel investors have helped to start up many distinguished companies, including Google and Alibaba. Both companies apparently have different names now, but the brand names resonate still. Angel investing is an alternative form of investing and usually occurs in a company's early stages of growth. I have always felt that there is a risk element from the point of view of the investor, but for a startup, this should be like a dream come true scenario. Because the angel investor wants you to succeed, they are normally open to offer mentoring or advice alongside capital. I would, if that gets me higher returns! Be prepared to part with some equity.

5. **Venture Capitalist**:

While angel investing is the go-to place for a startup looking for alternative forms of funding, the invested amounts are smaller and dwarf in comparison to the big boys, the venture capitalists. The big bets happen right here. Venture capitalists (VCs) are professionally managed funds who invest in companies that have scalability and growth potential. A venture capital would normally invest in a business against equity, just like an angel investor, but at higher valuation and stakes. The exit for an angel investor is usually when a venture capitalist comes on board while for a VC it is when there is an IPO or an acquisition. VCs provide expertise, mentorship and this is the stage where the effectiveness of your business is going to be put to test. Be prepared to be evaluated extensively and be tested rigorously from the sustainability and scalability point of view of your business. If you have achieved traction and generate revenues regularly, you are probably beyond the startup phase. this is when the VC investment may be appropriate for your business. Strong team would really matter at this stage so make sure you have the right group of individuals working for the same goals as you. Be prepared to be a little bit more flexible and sometimes give up a little bit more control.

6. **Incubators & Accelerators**:

    If you are at an early stage then there is a really good funding option for you in the form of Incubator and Accelerator programs. Universities, governments, networking groups are all working towards assisting start-ups, mostly in exchange of equity. You succeed, they succeed. what you do get is a great platform, normally a cohort, with infrastructure, tech and mentorship support to develop and scale. There isn't much difference in the two. Incubators hand hold you through the early stage providing infrastructure, training and networking, just like you would incubate an egg. Accelerators, more or less the same concept, but with more speed and result oriented direction, moving towards scalability. You would have to commit your time for these programs as they would normally run for almost 6 months. I do recommend incubators/accelerators because of the collateral connections with mentors, investors and other fellow start-ups who are associated with the same program.

So there you have it, five ways to raise funding for your startup. There are other ways you could look at like taking part in contests like hackathons, idea challenges, business plan competitions, etc. Winning contests can also get you some media coverage.

The crux of the matter is, however brilliant your idea or design, to really get your start-up take off to the skies, you will require capital. And if you are like most, not born with a golden spoon, you will need to raise funds. I have given you the ways to raise funds, but the whole process is riddled with frustration and anxiety. You would be like a newcomer actor giving an audition for a role in a movie, competition all around and at the mercy of the producer director, in our case the investor. It's not going to be easy for sure, but if you work on the fundamentals and understand the art of fundraising, you could definitely do better than others and have a distinct advantage. So, I am going to give you those fundamentals and advantage and hope you do well in your quest for funds.

Image by Pete Linforth of Pixabay

FUNDAMENTALS OF FUNDING

I have already outlined the various ways through which you can raise funds, but it is necessary to understand the flow, stages and the strategy behind fundraising. As I have mentioned before, the best way to start is bootstrapping. Let's call this stage Pre-Seed and would include funds raised from friends and family and of course your own funds. Use this stage of pre-seed to get your operations off the ground. The next stage is the Seed stage and refer back to Angel funding to understand what you need to do at this stage. This would be the stage where apart from getting your operations off the ground, you are also developing your product or MVP and doing market research. After the seed stage the start-up tree now starts to grow and would require more water and sunlight. This extra push comes in the form of Series A, B, C funding rounds. If you manage to reach this stage, be rest assured you have arrived. Most start-ups don't make it past the Seed stage. The last stage of the funding rounds after the Series A, B, C, D etc. is the ultimate goal of every start-up – being listed on the exchanges and launching an IPO. You get there and sky is the limit.

So, these are the rounds of funding. The basics remain the same in almost all rounds i.e., you would be offered funds in return for an equity stake in your business. The demands might change and be slightly different at each round, but the concept more or less remains the same.

Tool 21: Fundraising Strategy

Whatever the stage of your startup, whatever your fundraising goals, whatever the valuation of your company, you need to create a fundraising strategy. A fundraising strategy should outline the plan about raising funds. Just like you would do with a business plan and lean business model canvas I covered earlier, the fundraising strategy should be a concise one page document you use as a guideline. One page, concise, clear and you would be surprised how many valuable conversations and thought processes are derived from that. Of course, you need to do the groundwork in order to position yourself correctly in front of the right people.

For me the fundraising strategy, is based on your responses to these six questions:

1. Why are you raising capital?
2. Who are you raising the capital from?
3. When will you raise funds and timeline for the different stages?
4. How much capital will you raise at each stage?
5. How will you go about raising the funds?
6. How will you customize your plan for different investors?

Here's how you can go about answering these six questions.

1. **Why are you raising capital?**

   You need to start the whole process of making a fundraising strategy by first understanding the valuation of your company. Valuations are derived from many different factors, including your management, team, sales, traction, proven track record, market size, and the risk involved. Ideally, you should seek professional advice and services to calculate the valuation. A mistake often made by startups is that they look at a successful company in their space or industry and start valuating their own firm with the same benchmark. That needs to be avoided due to reasons I had mentioned before – critical mass, barrier to entry and moat. Create these and you can value your company higher, but till then be reasonable and not be greedy. Your valuation would also be a factor in the types of investors likely to get involved and the reasons why your company may be seeking new capital. When you become a going concern, the valuation methods would be mainly three (a) Discounted Cash Flow analysis, (b) Comparable Company and Industry analysis, and (c) Precedent transactions analysis.

   You need to understand, your reasons for raising capital and the valuation would be the right place to start. Once you have the valuation now try to find your reason for raising capital. Typically, the reason should come from one of these (a) Scaling faster (b) to gain credibility (c) resources (d) assistance with direction (e) generous funding terms. Understand your valuation, answer the "why" and move on to the next question.

2. Who are you raising the capital from?

   As I have covered earlier, there are multiple funding sources out there in addition to VC funding like angel investors, incubators/accelerators, crowd funding, bank loans, bootstrapping, and more. Your fundraising strategy should clearly outline all the planned funding sources. The sources would often be a progression all the way from bootstrapping to venture capital. Prior to your fundraising you should do a due diligence and research the investors you are going to raise from. Explore all options you have. You have to put a plan in place and do unbiased research to target the right investor and the right type of investment for your business.

Make sure the option you choose and the investors are the right fit in terms of your stage, your sector and ticket size. Don't compromise and be desperate just because you are getting some money. Choose investors who you feel, believe in you instead of seeking their capital blindly. You are offering a piece of your effort and hard work, make it count.

3. **When will you raise funds and timeline for the different stages?**

It is very important to set goals and time limits for your fundraising. Don't make that common mistake of going into fundraising blindly. Just because start-ups are known to be raising funds, does not mean that you have to. Every start-up has a unique requirement and timing for raising funds. So, the way to do this is by understanding the timing and amount by jotting down the reasons why you are raising funds, like, scaling, marketing, team building, research, development etc. Once you have a clear idea on why you are raising funds, it becomes easier for you to understand the timelines. Research and development would be earlier and scaling would be later. Set the milestones to hit for each round and it should be your endeavor to hit those milestones.

You must set clear, strategic, achievable, measurable goals and make them time specific for an effective fundraising plan. Raise when you are in a position of strength and not when you are just short of capital. Investors do not invest for credit shortages, rather they want to invest when they see an opportunity. Your main task should be to run an effective business and not raising funds, so keep a time limit on your fund raising activities and don't let it drag on for months on end. Ideally the stages should be 12-24 months part.

4. **How much capital will you raise at each stage?**

   In addition to knowing the stages for fundraising and the timelines for the same, it's important to know the amounts you're hoping to raise at each of these stages. The figures cannot be arbitrary, but should be based on facts and realistic assumptions. Like I said before, you should set specific milestones and the timelines should be such that you are able to forecast your funding requirements throughout the entire lifetime of your business. Greed can be a deterrent for most investors, so do not over-value your business and be blinded by optimism. Being optimistic is a good trait when it is within reason and achievable.

   The idea about knowing your stages and timelines is also very relevant for the amounts you raise as you should typically raise money based on what you would need to get to the next milestone of fundraising. Execution becomes a key, so make sure your ask and timelines are part of an achievable, measurable and believable plan.

5. **How will you go about raising the funds?**

   Your approach and management of your fundraising should be a process and a part of your overall plan. We make a fundraising strategy to use it as a guideline for our fundraising activities. Little tweaks and turns are always required as and when the situation demands or changes, but overall you need to have a concise plan in place. Your fundraising plan should clearly outline the outreach process for each investor based on which channel, timing and how you would go about it.

There are multiple tools available out there that make the process and planning a wee bit easier. Eprisa CRM, Luminate CRM, Blackbaud CRM are some examples of effective fundraising software CRMs you could use to streamline your fundraising operations and run them smoothly. Planning also would require you to be prepared. Have all the information and documents you need like pitch deck, cap table, KPIs, term sheets, financial model, contracts at hand along with the communication trail with each investor like your emails, meeting notes, reminders, etc.

6. **How will you customize your plan for different investors?**

    You and your business are unique, well, so is every investor. I have come across so many different investor personas in life and have been on the other side of the table too, shelling out funds in companies I believe in. I for one, love the story, the journey that brings an entrepreneur to the stage they are in, what matters to them. I still remember an investor who was with me in an angel investing group, who would only ask one question to everyone " Cap-table?". You will come across a lot of personalities, egos, prowess and those wielding tremendous knowledge, so be prepared.

    Some elders of my family started off in the tailoring business and I still remember what my Uncle Tochan told me of what makes a successful tailor – "bespoke".

You need to be like a bespoke tailor and customize your pitch to your investors, especially when it comes to creating a fundraising strategy that works. One-size-fits-all pitches just won't cut it.

Before meeting investors, make sure your investor pitch is polished and prepare 2-3 key points you are going to convey. Do an elevator pitch in your mind and that basically should cover your key points. Preparation is the key so try to learn about the investor you are going to pitch to, like you would learn about a company you apply for a job interview. Some key points will be the same for each investor, but the rest should be more customized. Every pitch you make should be a learning process for you and you should iron out the wrinkles in your pitch and deck after every meeting so you are polished and prepared for the next one. Prepare answers for any question or objection that may arise.

So there you have it, 6 solid questions answered to create a sturdy fundraising strategy. Before I sum it all up, I would like to cover a very relevant tool you as an entrepreneur are going to use extensively if you are raising funds, the Pitch Deck

Tool 22: The Pitch Deck

If you need to raise funding for your startup, you would need to create a pitch deck.

A pitch deck is a brief presentation, normally of 10-12 slides, that provides investors with an overview of your business and plan. A pitch deck should focus on showcasing your product or service, give insights into your business model, give the reader a look into your monetization strategy, and introduce your team.

I have compiled the 11 slides you should have in an effective pitch deck.

1. **Introduction and Vision**

   Introduce yourself and the reason you are pitching. Short and crisp.

2. **Problem**

   Define the problem, pain points and the need you are trying to solve

3. **Unique Value Proposition**

   Describe your solution and what makes your solution special and different from others.

4. **Product / Service**

   Showcase your product or service, how does it actually work, with examples.

5. **Team**

   Showcase your team and the skills each member brings on board and roles they play.

6. **Market**

   Show your knowledge and research of the potential and size of your target market.

7. **Milestones and Traction**

   Roadmap where you started, which stage you are at, and the traction you have achieved.

8. **Business and Revenue model**

   This should be about how you plan to make money and the revenue roadmap.

9. **Competition**

   Knowing your competition and the alternative solutions to the same problem is a must.

10. **Ask**

   What is your actual ask (for funds) and what kind of equity dilution are you offering in return.

11. **Funds use**

   Where and how would you be using the funds, define clearly, preferably draw a pie-chart.

So, these would be the 11 slides you would need for an effective pitch deck. Leave your contact details at the end. Remember to have extra slides with the important documentation like cap-tables, KPIs, term sheets, financial models, contracts, etc. What are you then waiting for then? Start making that awesome pitch deck and raise some funds!! Be creative and have clarity of concept.

Fundraising is an enduring, but a necessary part of the journey most startups take. Remember, with enough passion, perseverance and persistence – your fundraising milestones can be achieved, and that sense of achievement is just plain worth it!

> *"The most important thing is not to let fundraising get you down. Start-ups live or die on morale. If you let the difficulty of raising money to destroy your morale, it will become a self-fulfilling prophecy."*
>
> *– Paul Graham, Paul Graham Essays*

FUNDRAISING

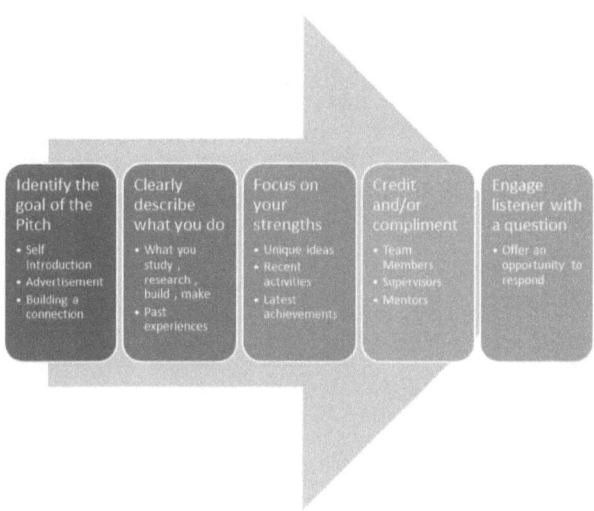

Illustration capd.mit.edu

TO SUM-UP

We have reached the end of this book and hopefully, it was insightful and would encourage you to get up and START-UP...JUST START-UP!! A lot of topics were covered in detail, from how to get an idea to its implementation, business plans, models, customers blueprints, productivity, marketing & sales, protection, scaling and raising funds. I loved writing about the digital marketing chapter as it is so relevant in today's scenario.

Having a startup and being an Entrepreneur will improve your standards of living and create wealth, not only for you but also for your Start-up. New markets are there to be developed and the ride of a lifetime awaits you.

All you have to do is get started and whenever you get stuck, you go back to the chapter of relevance and just read for clarity. I have put my heart and years of experience into this start-up guide for you ...hope it helps you in your entrepreneurial journey and you are super successful. Good Luck!!

TOOL LIST

Tool 1:	Do you have what it takes to be an entrepreneur? Test yourself.	PAGE 8
Tool 2:	Must have Skills of an Entrepreneur:	PAGE 12
Tool 3:	Know Yourself Chart – it starts here	PAGE 18
Tool 4:	The Right Mindset for Success	PAGE 21
Tool 5:	How to Get Ideas for Your Start-up	PAGE 29
Tool 6:	Validate your Business Idea	PAGE 41
Tool 7:	Minimum Viable Product – MV	PAGE 51
Tool 8:	Starting the Business Plan	PAGE 57
Tool 9:	The practical Business Plan	PAGE 59
Tool 10:	Understand Risk and Save money	PAGE 71
Tool 11:	Segment your Customers and make Buyer Persona	PAGE 82
Tool 12:	Customer Journey Map	PAGE 87
Tool 13:	Boosting Productivity	PAGE 96
Tool 14:	The Kanban Method	PAGE 100
Tool 15:	Marketing Strategy and Channels:	PAGE 109
Tool 16:	Sales & Lead Generation:	PAGE 113
Tool 17:	Seven pillars of Digital Marketing	PAGE 127
Tool 18:	Specialization and creating a niche:	PAGE 145
Tool 19:	Protect your Intellectual Property	PAGE 150

Tool 20:	Funding Options	PAGE 157
Tool 21:	Fundraising Strategy	PAGE 163
Tool 22:	The Pitch Deck	PAGE 168

SOME ADDITIONAL TOOLS:

Tool 23:	Some Great Ideas for a Startup	PAGE 39
Tool 24:	The Lean Canvas	PAGE 68
Tool 25:	The Kanban Board	PAGE 106
Tool 26:	Sales Pitch Template	PAGE 123

AUTHOR BIO

Gaurav Vasishta is an experienced Serial Entrepreneur and has launched 8 start-ups and had multiple successful exits over 22 years. His latest start-up is an Edtech firm "LeapWaters". An Angel investor, Gaurav has invested his funds in start-ups he believes in and has also been a Mentor to many more. An Educator, he has taught at many prestigious institutes and has given inspirational talks to entrepreneurs all over the world. His passion includes travel and linguistics. Following the same Gaurav has travelled to 43 countries and speaks 5 languages including Swedish and Thai.

Start-up...Just Start-up! is Gaurav's way of giving back to the start-up ecosystem. Coming from a humble background, he has had a long and an arduous entrepreneurial journey. He wants young entrepreneurs to benefit from his experience and genuinely wishes for them to be successful.

www.ingramcontent.com/pod-product-compliance
Lightning Source LLC
Chambersburg PA
CBHW020910180526
45163CB00007B/2694